WHAT GOD TOLD ME
TO TELL YOU

WHAT GOD TOLD ME TO TELL YOU

✦

The Three Essential Truths of Your Existence (Guaranteed Dogma-Free!)

Richard Hayes

iUniverse, Inc.
New York Lincoln Shanghai

WHAT GOD TOLD ME TO TELL YOU
The Three Essential Truths of Your Existence (Guaranteed Dogma-Free!)

iUniverse books may be ordered through booksellers or by contacting:

iUniverse
2021 Pine Lake Road, Suite 100
Lincoln, NE 68512
www.iuniverse.com
1-800-Authors (1-800-288-4677)

ISBN-13: 978-0-595-34008-8 (pbk)
ISBN-13: 978-0-595-78795-1 (ebk)
ISBN-10: 0-595-34008-3 (pbk)
ISBN-10: 0-595-78795-9 (ebk)

Printed in the United States of America

This book is dedicated to:
The person who gave me life: my mother, Mary;
The person who saved my life, Pete;
And the person who fills my life with love and laughter, my wife Jane.

A special acknowledgement
to my editor (and wife), Jane Salata: your sharp eye, pencil, and wit
have helped me immensely in writing this book. Thank you for all your
patience and encouragement.

Contents

FOREWORD

You'd never know it to look at him, or even from casual conversation with him, but Rich Hayes is truly all about God. And Rich's relationship with God is just that—a *relationship*, just like the everyday relationships that you and I have, complete with conversations, arguments, misunderstandings, re-understandings, love, anger, confusion, forgiveness. When Rich was a pre-schooler, his great wish was to be able to meet Jesus so that he could sit down and have a talk with Him. After a long and fruitless wait for the classic miraculous apparition, Rich set off on a winding spiritual path that has culminated in this relationship, and in the writing of this book.

When I met Rich many years ago, he was recovering from the breakup of his marriage and struggling to understand why all this had happened. He had incurred a number of great losses in his life: the death of a brother, financial peril, the loss of home and family. Yet he always kept his faith that his Higher Power had a greater plan, and that where understanding ended, faith and trust had to take over. At the time, I was a wan and lackluster agnostic. Whenever I would share with him my own frustrations and occasional despairing thoughts, he would always tell me, "It will all work out perfectly fine." As you can imagine, this was frustrating at best, and infuriating at worst. Only over time did I realize that this was the expression of Rich's profound gift of faith.

As spiritual teachers go, Rich is very self-effacing. He makes no bones about his personal "flaws," "failures," or "character defects." But, in keeping with his belief that "there are no mistakes in God's perfect world," he views these, as he views even the worst aspects of human existence, as holding the potential for learning, growth, and greater access to God.

It is this kind of acceptance that is at the core of this book. I hope you find it as accessible, as funny, as comforting and inspiring as Rich Hayes is himself.

Jane Salata

1

WHERE TO BEGIN?

I start to write and I hit a wall. What is it that God wants of me? Time and again this is my question. Yet I'd already been given an answer. I had already been told what I was to do. Then what was my problem? Doubt and fear. Doubt about my ability to do as instructed. Fear of what others might think. Fear that I might lose the comfortable life I was living. In doing what I was told to do, I would leave myself wide open to ridicule and, considering the current religious climate, maybe even hate. I might even get singled out by some of the same people who, following the September 11th tragedy, proclaimed that God was punishing us for homosexuality and abortion. Or perhaps the other side of that same coin: the people behind the flying of those jetliners. What I was told to do would leave me vulnerable, not an attractive option as far as I was concerned. I am a private person. To do what I was told might leave me open to any of these things. So the truth is, I don't want to do this, period.

Yet I know I must. But how? So I ask for help, appeal for guidance: "Please help me to let go of all these fears I have and do what you asked of me—use me—my hands, my mind—give me the right words so that people will understand….". And I begin to type once more. But there's that wall again. Wham! I hit it. I'm stopped in mid-sentence. Where did the words go? I wait, but nothing happens. On my computer screen the cursor sits, waiting patiently for me to continue. But I can't. There are no words. Why can't there be an easier way to do this??? So here on a frigid morning in February of 2004, I finally give up. I have no choice. Try as I might, I'm finally ready to admit that there is no other way to do what I've been trying to do so unsuccessfully. So I surrender.

This whole thing started for me a few years earlier, and ever since it happened I've been trying to figure a way to do as I was told. That is, once I finally accepted that my experience had been real. You see, God gave me a message. So, that being said, you can probably understand why I've been trying to find a way to do what I was told to do, without saying "Who" it was that told me. That's the "safe" way I've been looking for. I've tried over and over again to find a way to deliver the message I received on that day without telling the story of what happened. Obviously I've not been very successful. What you have here in your hands is the result of my failure to find another way to do this thing.

When this happened to me, I was going through a tough time. Not that things were bad for me, because they weren't. If anything, they were quite the opposite. What I'm referring to here is my state of mind at the time, not my life circumstances. I was very happily married to a wonderful woman I'd met 9 years earlier. I had a nice home and lived in a place I loved, had 3 healthy kids, two of whom were grown and on their own. For over a half dozen years I'd been able to do something I loved: play music. I'd also been able to quit working at a career I'd found unrewarding and tedious the same said years. Things were good—very good. So how was this spot "tough" for me? Well, my answer will probably not elicit much sympathy from you. It was tough because things _were so good_. You see, I felt guilty with a capital "G". Not that I felt guilty all of the time, but when it surfaced it could be terrible, at times almost overwhelming. And when this happened my mind would take off on me, running down a long list of things I _should_ be doing. This was one of those times.

Where had I learned to have such guilt? Catholic school? Or maybe the fact that I was alive and my younger brother wasn't? Who knows? But I do know that on this day in October of 2001 I was asking myself where I was going and what was I doing to get there? And there seemed no clear answer. I felt adrift and rudderless—as if I had no direction in life. Of course this was not true, but it *felt* true to me. I'd been through this before—many times in fact. But I'd never been 48 years old before. This was a place and an age I'd never imagined for myself. It was the realm of my parents and other "older folks"—how the hell could I be this old and not know what I'm doing??? And with the lack of any clear answers I felt only more guilt. How did I deserve to have it so good while so many others didn't? What had I done that they hadn't? Or was it even about that? Was it just the cards I'd drawn, the way the dice fell? An accident of birth, because I'd wound up with parents who'd been pretty well off?

But I don't want to mislead you. I had not skipped along through life without my share of pain or failure. I was well acquainted with these. As a matter of fact, they traveled together. And as far as my life was concerned, they were like the German trains—extremely punctual, showing up every six years. The pattern was the same: I'd know what I wanted and would have a plan to accomplish it. I'd work hard, doing whatever I believed was needed. Within a few years I'd usually be doing okay, and the struggle part would seem to be over. Things would be going well. But then something always seemed to happen. I'd begin to see the need for a change of some kind. My attitude would shift. Mental clouds would gather. I'd become a bit bored, then restless and uneasy. In the final stage I'd become totally negative, believing the "problem" was in whatever it was I was doing, and that no options existed other than starting all over in a completely different direction. This pattern had made for an eclectic career track. There had been three of these cycles in my adult life. The first one coming to a close in 1979 with the ending of a moderately successful career in music. Then in 1985 with the loss of a business I had started after that music career, and finally in 1991, when a whole series of things piled up on me, not the least of which was the loss of a well paying job. Clearly there was a progression going on, with the ending of each cycle being more painful than the previous one. In 1991 I began to suspect a pattern. That's when I started to connect the dots, although I wasn't quite sure what they connected to. Only that they were all somehow related. But once I got this, seeing that there was a relationship, my life began to change. It was as though that recognition catapulted me forward, bringing new people and experiences to me, and bringing an end to this pattern of six year cycles. There had been no crash, no chaotic slide into crises in ten years; only the usual ups and downs that life hands us all. Perhaps that was the guilt I was feeling?

The end of that last cycle in 1991 had in fact been the worst of all. Having accumulated more in my life, there was much more to lose. At the time it had seemed like the end of the world to me, and I guess you could say that in a way it was. At least the end of the world I had believed existed. My 18 year marriage ended abruptly, I felt the sting and humiliation of being fired, I lost my home, partially lost my kids to an ugly divorce struggle, and I lost my mother to dementia. Now mind you, these things all happened within months of one another. Each one had blind-sided me. I'd had no hint of any trouble in the marriage, in my mom's health, or that I'd find myself unemployed and remain so for several months. That was 1991 for me. A year that only went one way: from bad to worse.

But, all that was well behind me by the day I got this message. Things in my life had worked out better than I ever would have believed possible back then. As terrible as that time had been for me, it had also been one of the major turning points of my life. It had gotten my attention. The pain was the wake up call, the bucket of ice water poured over my head, the thing that finally made me willing to try doing things differently in my life. Oftentimes we don't realize we've hit a turning point until years later when we look back. But that hadn't been the case for me in 1991. I stood at a crossroads and knew it. After all, it's pretty hard to miss your life falling apart. But this was not the case in 2001 when I received this message. I didn't see the turn I'd come to. When this thing happened I knew it was significant, I just didn't know where it would lead me—or how. I'd been feeling myself on some sort of spiritual quest, as though I was being "called"—I just wasn't sure by who, or to what. I guess you could say I'd been calling out as well—I just hadn't expected the kind of answer I got.

As I said a moment ago, watching your life fall apart can be a compelling incentive to change the way you do things. And that's exactly what I'd done. How I lived my life post 1991 was quite different then pre 1991, and I attributed the vast improvement in my life circumstances since then in no small part to that fact. By 2001 I'd been practicing both prayer and meditation on a daily basis for years, although I followed no formal practice for either beyond simply sitting quietly and calming my mind. I had not returned to any church, nor had I embraced any religious view. My prayers were simple things, "thank you" being my favorite. On that day I couldn't see what this experience would do to the next few years for me. I had no way to know that it would send me reeling and struggling, questioning and doubting. At times I'd be filled with a sense of overwhelming trust, absolutely certain in what I must do. Yet only a few hours later I'd be back at fear, doubt and denial, second guessing myself as well as this experience. I have at times felt almost tormented by the decision of whether to go "public" or not. And, just as I had no idea of what I was in for the day that this happened to me, I have no way of knowing how this will turn out. Perspective only goes one way.

Before we go any further I want to get a few things straight. I do not believe I've been chosen by God. At least no more than any of us are chosen. I also want to talk for a moment about my doubts around this experience before I tell you what happened. When this thing occurred I didn't know what to make of it. I did not immediately accept that it was a message from God. Because of the nature of the experience I initially felt that I must have made it up or imagined it. It was not a booming voice from above. It was not a burning bush. It was not a white light illuminating the notebook page in front of me. The sun didn't fall from the sky. The heavens did not open up. There was no celestial choir. Nothing around me changed—or so I thought. So after it happened I said nothing. I told no one, not even my wife Jane. How do you tell someone that you received a message from God the other day, especially when you're not even sure you believe it yourself? I was familiar with the so-called phenomenon of "automatic writing", which is said to be channeling intelligence from the spiritual realm. But truthfully, while I found the idea intriguing, I had also been pretty skeptical. I guess I thought it might be possible, but I also thought it might be a lot of hogwash. And I never for the life of me expected it to happen to me. That is a very large part of what I've struggled with.

But I do have the notebook I traveled to that hillside with, the one that contains six pages of questions and answers. I have referred to it often as I've struggled with writing this book. These things, written in my own hand, have taken on deeper meaning for me with the passage of time. As I go over them, and over them, I begin to see more meaning, to understand in deeper ways what I was told that day. The message I got was not terribly complex. If anything it was painfully simple. I say "painful" because of all the suffering that's happened in our world because we misunderstood three key things. Had we accepted these three things, today's world would not exist. A far better one would. I also got a few personal questions answered—some things that had been troubling me for a long time. While they were answered, at the time they weren't answered to my satisfaction. Simply put: I didn't get it. Some of it seemed a bit like double talk. It's some of those answers I referred to a moment ago when I described a deeper meaning being understood as time passed and I read and re-read what I'd written. Everything takes time. And that's exactly what has been needed for me to get to this point: lots of time—and a whole sh*t-load of writing!

So here's the story of what happened that day. It was a Tuesday in early October 2001, only a few weeks after 9/11. I had been working at home in my office and, as you already know, was giving myself a hard time over decisions I felt I needed to make. As I grappled with the notion of whether to take a job or continuing to work for myself, the only conclusion I was able to arrive at regarded a cup of coffee, and my need for one. I set out for my local coffee shop to grab a cup and take a ride to a favorite spot of mine, an overlook by a nearby lake. The day was a picture perfect autumn day in New England, golden sunlight and brilliant blue skies. On a day like this it was hard to imagine that anything could be wrong in the world. But all of us knew there was. Less than two hundred miles south of me rescue workers were still removing bodies from the wreckage where the towers had stood. I'd taken a notepad with me so I could write out some ideas for the future. I also began a list of my personal strengths and weaknesses, separating the page into a plus and minus column. The list of personal qualities began to fill the right side of my page. That was the place for my negatives. As I looked down at them I felt those all too familiar pangs of guilt digging in deeper. I put the pen down. I felt as though I was about to burst, a mixture of frustration and despair. My list making had given me nothing new. It was just more of the same old, recycled stuff I'd been running around in my head for years: do this—try that. I was being overtaken by the "what ifs?", and "how will's?", and of course the ever popular "who are you kidding! Who do you think you are anyway...". I felt myself on the verge of tears. What the hell was I really doing with my life anyway? I wanted to scream. But I didn't. Instead I sat there.

I'm not sure how much time passed as I did this. But at some point I realized I'd taken the pen back in hand because I noticed I was mindlessly doodling. Then, for no reason other than—well truthfully I can't tell you what my reasoning was, because I simply don't remember. Whatever the reason, below my scribbles I wrote a question. It was the question that had me so frustrated, the one that made me want to scream out. I wrote it to God. It was a question whose answer had been eluding me all those years: what am I *supposed* to be doing? That's when "it" happened. Instantly an answer came back. My hand never paused after putting the dot under the question mark. Moving in one fluid motion, the pen seemed to choose the words needed. I looked down and read what I'd just scribbled out onto that paper. There was the answer to my question. It said what I was supposed to do. But what the hell had just happened? Was it me who gave that answer? It certainly didn't seem that way. I mean, yes, it was my hand that held the pen. But I had no awareness of thinking the words that my hand wrote. I decided to try it again, and to really pay attention this time. I sat still for a moment, thinking about what else I wanted to know. I wrote my next question. The same thing happened. When I finished dotting the question mark, the pen kept going. The words came pouring out. Again I had the sense that the pen itself was thinking them. This give and take continued until it filled six sheets of paper at the back of my notebook. So, on that beautiful October afternoon, I was told I had a job to do and a message to deliver. I was told that I've always known this message, that I'd understood it before I understood anything else in this world. That was my job: deliver it. And as suddenly as it had begun, it was over. I wrote another question but nothing happened. Apparently there was no more that needed to be said. The rest was now up to me. I sat there in the bright afternoon sunshine and re-read the things I'd just written. A sense of unreality began to set in, as if it had all been a dream. In a matter of only minutes I made the leap to doubt. I must have made it up. It must have been some kind of trick from my subconscious mind, my deeply suppressed wishes and desires spilling out. After all, why would God speak to me this time, as opposed to all the other times I'd needed answers and help—times that were certainly more compelling. At least as far as I was concerned. Perhaps a little history on my relationship with God might be in order at this point. I promise to keep it brief.

As a small child I'd felt as if I knew God personally. As a matter of fact, some of my earliest memories are of my feelings toward, and from, God. It was trust, absolute and complete. God was completely loving and accepting, and I felt personally held and cared for. Then I went to school. The God I heard about there didn't sound like the same one I knew. A lot of the stories made God sound angry and unreasonable, even a bit crazy—especially when He asked a guy to kill his own son just to prove his obedience. Thankfully, God called that one off at the last minute. But what about all the other stuff? Plagues, famine, floods! The slaughter of the innocents! I learned that some really bad things happened to good people. But then it got even worse, because those good people were now good people I knew—people like my best friend in the first grade, Vinny, who along with his sisters, brothers and mother, died in a house fire one cold Saturday morning in January. And then, a few years later, my pain-in-the-ass little brother died of cancer at the ripe old age of nine. All the prayers said by tons of good people didn't stop it from happening. All the special Masses offered up on his behalf didn't stop it from happening. The blessed water brought back from Lourdes and rubbed on his scarecrow body didn't stop it from happening. And (probably most significant to me, considering the closeness I'd always felt with God), my own appeals didn't stop it from happening. Clearly God wasn't listening. Or worse yet, didn't care. At this point I realized on a very deep level that bad stuff happened all the time to innocent kids. Children perished not only in death camps and firestorm bombings because a war was going on, but also at the hands of murderers and rapists. And of course as a result of diseases like cancer. By the so-called age of reason, I'd reasoned that something didn't add up regarding God. Then I went one step further, and began doubting the existence of *a God* altogether. That almost seemed better. It was easier to understand. After all, what sort of God would allow such injustices and suffering?

But my atheism didn't last very long. By the end of my teen years I decided maybe I'd been a bit rash. There had to be something to God, and so I went looking. I tried a few different churches, heard some charismatic preachers and wanted desperately to believe what they had to say. Then I saw some church politics up close and personal, and had some strong second thoughts about the whole deal. Finally I came to the conclusion that if the only way to find God was in a church then I wouldn't be finding Him anytime soon. And who said it really was a Him, anyway? I walked away from all formal churches, taking my questions (and doubts) about God along with me.

But the birth of my first child finally put to rest any remaining doubts about the existence of God. What else could explain such a miracle? Surely it was much more than merely biology that I saw when I first gazed into those newborn eyes and saw consciousness looking back at me. This returned me to an acceptance of *a* God. But acceptance is not synonymous with relationship. I *knew* that something was there, but I really had no idea what that might be. And that's were it stayed for years. I didn't really pray at all. To me, God was out "there" some-where, doing whatever it was that God did. There was nothing at all personal about it.

This lasted until the end of that last 6 year cycle. In the final months of 1991 it seemed I had no place else to go. I turned to God and I began to pray, this despite conclusions reached in my earlier life that prayer didn't work because it never had seemed to. But I was desperate, so I asked for help. And that's exactly what I got. Why this time and not the other times—the times when I'd secretly and silently prayed "Please God, help me! Save my business", or "please help me get the money we need for these bills", or "help me pass", "make them well", and the ever popular "please, oh please don't let them catch me…"? And how about all the other pleas I'd tried throughout the years? Well, today I believe those prayers were answered. I had been helped, just not in the way *I'd* wanted. Help doesn't necessarily mean an absence of pain or an avoidance of consequences. But more on that later. I believe the results were so apparent to me in 1991 because of my expectations when I prayed. Unlike practically all my prayers of the past, these prayers did not ask for a specific outcome. It was simply "Please help me. You know what is best, so please do what is best for me and every-one concerned". And here is the key, although I didn't know it at the time. I not only <u>believed</u> things *would* work out—I knew they would. How did I know? I can't tell you that. But I did—just as surely as I knew anything. I trusted completely that I'd be taken care of. And I was. Totally unforeseen and unimagined events began to line up in my life. No, things didn't get better immediately—at least not "out there" in the world around me. But on the inside it was a different story. This certainty—this "knowing" I felt—was Grace. I have no other explanation for such a shift in my ability to trust something unseen and unknown. This kind of trust had been totally out of the question for me. I'd learned very early in my life not to trust. After all, my own parents couldn't protect my little brother, and God certainly didn't protect all those people who'd died so horribly. That's why I say this was Grace, because it is perfectly clear to me that I did not bring about this change within me. As my inside world became transformed, so to did my outside world begin to change. And finally, those changes and the course my life had taken through the following decade, allowed me to be on that hillside that day, pen in hand and notebook open.

So, after a lot of back and forth arguments with myself I finally concluded that the experience was real. I based this on one compelling piece of evidence: there was no way that the things written by my hand originated in my mind. I didn't even understand what some of them meant! But I still refused to tell anyone. So then the challenge to me became how I would do this thing—how I'd deliver this message. That's where you came in at the very beginning. Those words of frustration were my final pleadings as I had just trashed my umpteenth attempt at writing a book that, in the finally analysis, simply and crudely put: sucked! That's what has finally pushed me over the edge! I guess I needed to be convinced. There is no other way to do this thing. After all, why it is so difficult for me to say that I am doing God's bidding? Or that God would speak to me? Today I believe God does speak, not only to me, but to all of us. And it's happening all the time. It's just that we miss it or doubt it most of the time. Maybe my own struggle with this comes from all the people I see who claim to be doing God's bidding as they blow themselves and others up. Or maybe it comes from my long ago fear of being made fun of. I guess the sting of ridicule, although almost a half century old, still has some bite to it. But I must let that go. And I must let go of what you or anyone else chooses to think about me. After all, it's not about me—it's about the message.

The book that follows is based on the things I was told that day. It has helped me to understand why things are the way they are right now. But more importantly, it's about what <u>we can do to change them</u>.

I have had no other such experiences since that day. However, at times when I am writing here and looking for a way to say something, if I'm able to let go and get out of my own way, then something does happen. And then I get to have the experience of wondering: who said that? As you already know, I'm a musician. My main instrument is lead guitar. I can only compare this experience of the right words showing up, as if of their own accord, to what happens on occasion when I'm playing. As a lead guitarist I get to improvise some of the solos I play. Most times I have a basic idea of what I'm going to do. But every so often I like to take a chance—be totally daring. That's when I throw out any notion of what I want to play. It's a little like working the trapeze without a net. I let go and dive into the nothingness! Then something happens. I have no thought about it, it just happens. I've heard some of these solos played back on recordings and couldn't believe my ears. Why? Well, in all honesty, I don't know how to do some of the things I've heard played back. Yet there they are, captured on tape. I'm not saying I can't play a decent solo, because after all these years I certainly hope I can. But I do know my limitations. At least I thought I did. But quite obviously something does happen when we get out of our own way. So that is my wish throughout this book.

Please note :To make things easier to read I have separated the text and used bold italics when conveying what I was told that day on the hillside. Hopefully this will be helpful to you.

2

The Message

o o o o o o o o o o o o o o o o o o o o o o o o o o o o o o o o o o

You are totally worthy. You are totally loved. Nothing can ever separate you from God

If we all believed these three things, the world would be a very different place. But you *did* know this once. Believe it or not, a part of you still does—it's just not the part you're usually in touch with. Who you think you are has forgotten. Who you believe yourself to be has bought into something else entirely. Practically all of us have forgotten what is true, and believed what isn't. In place of the truth we've substituted something that's caused a ton of suffering and pain. It's a belief that somehow or in someway we are "not worthy". This phrase became a comic punch line made famous on Saturday Night Live and in the movie "Wayne's World" back in the 1990's. We all laughed, probably because we all could identify. Deeply hidden in most of us there resides a groveling nerd who feels undeserving to be in the presence of greatness, wanting desperately to be liked and accepted, hoping that by such close proximity he may gain a bit of status himself. Any time you've felt inferior, less than, not good enough, or undeserving, this belief has been active. Believing this has caused you to feel alone, isolated, different, "apart from" rather than "a part of". At times it's caused you to lash out and hurt others, sometimes intentionally, but usually not. It's a belief that has given birth to that negative and at times cruel voice in

14

your head, the one that is usually ready to pounce on you, reminding you that you really don't measure up. Of the three statements above, the misunderstanding of this first one is what makes two other major mistakes possible: that you need to do something to be loved, and that you are alone and on your own, separate from the Divine. This is absolutely not true!

How did such a huge misunderstanding get started? And, more importantly, how did it spread to "infect" practically all of humanity? Simply put, our ancestors arrived at a wrong conclusion a very long time ago. Despite some very enlightened and gifted teachers coming along throughout history to tell us otherwise, a good many of us continued staying with what we "knew". The story of humanity's fall from grace is one of the myths originally created to describe the forgetting that happens when we are born into this world. But we got the rest of that story wrong. As the great teacher and mythologist Joseph Campbell said, we got stuck in the metaphor. We believed it as fact. We took the interpretation as literal: we'd been cast out and this necessitated our "earning" our way back. This set up the whole dynamic of us "here" and God "there". And eon upon eon of believing this, or some variation of it, has created the world today. But what we see is not real. What, then, is real? Let me explain.

While we are physical beings, that is not all that we are. We are also Spirit. Everything that exists in this supposedly material world has its origins in Spirit. We are now, at this moment, experiencing being human. But behind this is our true Self, and it is Eternal. While at our deepest level, the core of Who we are, we do know this, we rarely go there—at least not in our so-called "waking" state. It remains unknown territory to most of us. At times we do get some sense of this when it starts to bubble up into our consciousness and we get a "feeling" of some sort—a sense that we are part of something so much bigger than what we see. But usually it gets brushed aside by the preoccupations of our day to day life. The world we see as we peer out from our physical bodies fools us, because most of us believe it is the real world. That point could be argued as to what constitutes "real" but I'm not planning to do that here. Let's just say that the world we see is "real" in only a very small spectrum of what is real. We see only a tiny portion of what is there. To believe it is actual reality might be like comparing it to our going to the movies and believing that the images we see on the screen are real. In one sense the images are, but that is very limited. They are mere projections, and only a crazy person would believe that they constituted actual "reality". But isn't that what many of us do when we limit ourselves to believe in only what we can see, touch, taste, hear or smell? Many more things lie unseen than seen. We've created countless instruments that confirm this. If we don't see them do they exist? Of course they do. Before we invented the instruments, did they exist? You see my point. I tell you these things in order that you might open your mind to some of the things I'll be talking about here.

Let's back up for a minute to what I just mentioned about your true nature being eternal. How can I say such a thing? After all, there has been no conclusive scientific proof. There are hundreds, if not thousands, of documented cases of what have come to be called "near death experiences". But many in the medical and scientific community do not recognize these as proof. So it's generally agreed that we simply don't know. So how is it that I can say what I've said with such conviction? Well, I'm not the One saying it. Did you catch the capital letter I used on "one"? That's the source of this information. It's actually contained in the third sentence of the message: Nothing can (or will) ever separate you from God. You cannot get more definite that that! Nothing. No "thing". Nothing and no thing can ever separate you from God. God, which is That which is eternal. You cannot be separated from That which always is. So there you have it from the Source: your Source, <u>our</u> Source. Of course, whether you believe this or not is totally up to you. But then again, so is everything else in your life.

Aside from the message that opened this chapter, there is no more important message in this book then what has just been told to you in those last two sentences: Your life is up to you. If you take nothing else from this book—if you never turn another page of it—I urge you to take this. You see, we are involved in how our lives, and all life, unfolds, in ways most of us never imagined. This, despite what you may think. But even more importantly, <u>because </u>of what you do think!! Thoughts are not just wisps of the immaterial, they are real "things" and they connect you and your consciousness to the realm from which you and everything else originates.

Let me caution you: some of what you're about to read may in fact disturb you. It may, and probably will, run counter to the way you believe (think) the world works. If you consider yourself to be an innocent bystander as you watch what goes on around you, then prepare to be disturbed. If you've believed that the world's problems are so huge that you are powerless to do anything to change things, then prepare to be surprised. And, if you've often hoped or believed that someone else (a politician, a great leader, a fabulous doctor, a brilliant scientist, a genius inventor, a saint, or the Savior Himself)would come along and solve these problems, fixing this damned mess once and for all, prepare to be disappointed. If you've been locked into a belief of the way things really work and are, then what you are about to read may be difficult for you. But I hope you will allow yourself to be disturbed or uncomfortable. You are about to find out how much you have to do with the way things are in the world. That's right: you and the world are both tied together—linked in ways you can hardly imagined. To borrow from an oft-used phrase regarding politics: all life is local. And the good news is you get to have a say in the way things turn out here.

What? You're saying you don't want that kind of responsibility? Well, then, I've got some bad news for you. Your life and all its circumstances, the world and all its confusion and struggle, everything that you currently see and experience will keep on keeping on. If that's okay for you and you're satisfied with that answer, then close this book and either give it away, or put it someplace where you'll be able to find it when you've finally had enough pain. Am I saying that what you learn here will get rid of pain in your life? God forbid!!! How would you ever learn anything! This book will not eliminate pain. But it can help you to transform your pain and, by that, your life.

If you've decided to hang with me and continue on here, then I have a suggestion for you: become willing to let go of answers you've assumed to be true. This doesn't mean they're not true. It simply means you're willing to take another look. Try to become willing to "not know". To "not know" can be a very good thing, despite what most of us learn through school, work, or the world. When we're able to admit we don't know a thing, we become "open". We create space. But remember this : answers can (and do) change. What was once "correct" may no longer be.

Let's return to the B—I—G mistake we've believed in: unworthiness. What a mess it's created in both ourselves and our world. This belief has been like a song playing continually in the background of our subconscious mind. Like a broken record, playing the same messages over and over again. We've been marching to a tune we can't hear—but we feel it's beat. And it is at the very root of our troubles in this world.

Believing this we have no choice but to believe we are flawed and undeserving in some way. But you may be saying to yourself that you don't presently believe this at all, that it's just some old fashioned religious nonsense you gave up believing a long time ago. What if you happen to be agnostic or atheist, and never believed such a thing? Well, none of those things matters. You've gotten the message anyway, and it's still in there, mixed in with all the other things swimming around in that vast ocean of your unconscious. You see, it's part of the memory of our species, stored in what Carl Jung referred to as our collective unconscious. This buried belief of unworthiness is pandered to and reinforced by Madison Avenue, as they sell us whatever it is they need to sell. It is practically impossible for us to escape them and the messages they convey. According to Adbusters of Vancouver Canada, the average American is subjected to over 3000 advertisements a day! That is a staggering amount of information. And even more troubling is the staggering amount of negative reinforcement the message that you are in some way lacking! Advertising has raised the delivery of this message to high art. It's always about what you don't have, what you need, and how much better you'll be once you've gotten it. But of course, then there's always the "next" thing you "need". Our very economy is built upon this fallacy. And believe me when I tell you that there's an awful lot of money riding on most of us continuing to believe this.

Okay, so you can see how having this unconscious belief plays into the advertisers' hands. But aside from pushing some of us into debt as we try to buy the solution to our problem, how does it cause trouble out in the world? After all, by believing this aren't we mainly harming our selves? Well, if it stopped right there, then the answer would be yes. But it doesn't. That's just the tip of the iceberg. Why? Because of all the other things we do in order to avoid this hidden belief. And because it is unconscious we don't even know that we're doing anything! We don't recognize that this is the driving force as it operates without our knowledge. We act and behave in ways that we believe make sense and are necessary. But what's motivating us is something we're oblivious to.

This is not to say that we are totally clueless about our feelings of being less-than or unworthy. Each one of us has times when we're very much in touch with not feeling good enough in some way. Nor does it mean we're ignorant about choosing to believe in our unworthiness, or that we must earn God's love and acceptance. These may even be the tenets of the faith we've embraced. For far too many of us, this is something we've been taught and believe very deeply. So if anything, it is quite conscious because, after all, as far as we're concerned it is the truth. But here's the thing: even if we are conscious of this choice, we're in the dark about what's going on behind the scenes. That's because of a coordinator that orchestrates things for us. You may have heard of it: the ego. Now the ego has taken its share of knocks in recent years, becoming almost a bad word to many. It's very hip to try and "go beyond the ego" these days. After all, according to many, the ego is the cause of so many of our difficulties and struggles. There's no question that an ego run amok is not something many of us enjoy being around. But the ego does have a job to do: integration. However the trouble I'm speaking about here stems from one of the ego's other functions: protection. But it's not so much the protection, as what the ego is trying to protect, that really stirs things up. The ego believes it is you. Furthermore, you believe it is you as well!

Although the word "ego" is tossed about pretty freely these days, perhaps a brief overview of what it is (and does) might help to clarify things a bit. The ego is defined as the portion of the psyche experienced as the "self" or "I." It is the part of us that remembers, evaluates, plans, and in other ways is responsive to and acts in the surrounding physical and social world. According to Sigmund Freud, it coexists with the id (the unconscious, instinctual portion of the psyche) and the superego (the portion representing the conscience, or the internalization of societal norms—a kind of internalized parent). The ego serves to integrate these and other aspects of the person, such as memory, imagination, and behavior. It mediates between the id and the superego by building up various defense mechanisms. I draw your attention to those last two words "defense mechanisms". Remember, the ego is defined as the part "experienced" as the "I" or self. I call it the "small -s self". It is not you. It is no more you than your hand is you. Both are simply parts of you used by you here in this life.

Lets back up to the "defense" section of our definition, because here's the trouble in a nutshell. What the ego does in order to protect you is to try and do away with anything that it sees as detrimental to you. As far as it's concerned, a belief in unworthiness is just that. In order to get rid of this it projects it (just like a movie camera showing a film at the theatre) and the feelings associated with it, out onto the world and other people, and that becomes where we "see" these qualities. They're bad, or wrong, or stupid, or evil. And yes, sometimes this may be the truth. They may be all those things and more. But even if that is true, it is only a tiny piece of a much greater truth. And let's not forget: these other people who we believe are the problem are basically doing the same thing we are! Driven by their own personal agendas as well as their own personal version of unworthiness. The difficulty and the problem is always in that "other," and to each of us there are hundreds, thousands, even millions of "others" to choose from. Things won't be better until they're dealt with or gotten rid of. And we really, really, believe this. We have no idea that we're doing it based on something inside of us that we can't stand! This is a very basic example of what's been happening over and over again for thousands of years and in billions of lives. The trouble out there in the world is born within each of us. For the purposes in this book, when I refer to the ego it is what has been described here. I'll also be calling this the small letter "s" self. Let's continue.

There can be a problem with the projection of our movie. Some of it doesn't make it out on to the screen of the world. What do we do with the un-projected stuff? Well, what the ego isn't successful at getting rid of "out there" gets stored away back down in the subconscious mind. So in essence, we know about it but we don't know we know about it. And that creates other problems for us because the ego wants to keep us from finding this stuff. It's the old "out of sight—out of mind" trick. Well, sort of. This is where unhealthy behaviors and addictions can come into the picture. In part they are driven by the need to avoid whatever we might find out if we start digging. Doesn't the ego "know" this isn't good for you? After all, if it thinks it is you, shouldn't it want what's best for you? Well, to the ego protection against being uncomfortable *is* what's best. It's job is to protect. All the ego knows is that it doesn't feel good. The ego can be a bit like a two year old in some ways. And in the early stages of many of these behaviors and actions we do feel good, sometimes even great. Or so we think. But as we take this path as a solution, more and more, it is this "two year old" who is driving the car. Sounds pretty risky, doesn't it? Yet we go along with all this because it "helps" us to escape this terrible "truth" about our self—only we don't know it.

We spend money we don't have and rack up debt. We jump from relationship to relationship. An occasional drink after work becomes a nightly habit, and then more. We discover the thrill of online auctions, or pornography. Or, maybe the status of financial success is the solution to this unease we feel with our self and our world. Anything that will keep us on the move, running, grasping, and chasing. What I'm describing here is some of what has given the ego its bad reputation. If the tail *is* wagging the dog, then we've got a problem. When any of these things is occurring that is precisely what's going on. Egomania: often unrecognized, but very much in charge of our actions. And egomania does not have to exhibit itself in conceit and arrogance. Egomania also shows up as self-loathing. Egomania is the operative word whenever it refers to obsession with the small "s" self. How can someone who hates themself be an egomaniac? Simple. That's all they think about.

Okay, but where am I going with all this? Well, my hope is that I'm causing you to think about these things and how they apply to you. Being aware of this is taking the first step. But simply knowing this doesn't change things a whole lot. You will continue to do these things. Even if you accept everything I've said here as 100% true, you will still do them. But maybe a little less often. Maybe you'll catch yourself the next time you're ready to pronounce another person a problem. Maybe instead of reacting to something without thinking, next time you will pause and ask yourself why you're about to do what you're about to do. I like to call this the sacred pause. I recommend practicing it often. And when you forget, remind yourself to do it the next time the opportunity presents itself, because it will. This is a gradual process, but it is the start of great change. It is the beginning of becoming conscious.

The truth is that you have been programmed, much as a computer is programmed. But there is a bug in the program. And this programming is stored in your subconscious mind. The subconscious is more like a computer than most of us realize. It does not practice discernment, does not weigh the validity of what it is fed. It takes it as fact. And although you've been unaware that this belief in unworthiness has been there, it has been operating in the background all this time. And it has affected you deeply. But now you <u>do</u> know, and you do have a choice. Let the following statement burn itself into your consciousness:

No matter what you've done in your life, it cannot change this. You may have behaved in ways that were totally and absolutely *unworthy of your true nature, but that is <u>behavior</u> and not <u>you</u>—it's what you've <u>done</u>, not who you <u>are</u>. Accepting this will change your life in ways hardly imaginable to you at this moment. Forgive yourself. There is no more important act than forgiveness. Practice it on yourself so you may practice it with others.*

So far we've talked about what unworthiness has done to us individually, and we've gotten an idea of its effect on people we come into contact with. Now let's look at the bigger picture: society and the current world situation. Open today's newspaper and scan the headlines and stories. Of course, I have no way of knowing what they will really be on this particular day as you're reading this. After all, I've written this early in the year of 2004. Nevertheless, I'll venture a few guesses: somewhere someone has just blown up a car or building. Somewhere there's a new terrorist threat. Somewhere two nations are edging closer to war. Somewhere else a bloody war is getting even bloodier. Somewhere there's been a political coup. Somewhere a scandal has been uncovered, leading to the highest offices of government. Somewhere a major corporation that has always been considered "rock solid" is suspected of cooking the books. Somewhere it's suspected that genocide may be taking place. Somewhere there's been a senseless and violent murder. Somewhere there's been a brutal rape. Somewhere someone has been beaten and tortured. Somewhere a country is being swept by famine, but a large amount of the emergency supplies have found their way to the black market instead of people's mouths. Somewhere a factory has moved and people are losing thousands of jobs to somewhere else. Oh, yeah, I almost forgot: somewhere someone is claiming that God is on their side as they fight against an "evil" enemy.

So, how did I do? Nothing would please me more than for all headlines like these to be something only found in history books. I believe that will happen someday. But first we must get through this time in order that these things be relegated to history. Behind each of these incidents and situations is the ignorance and denial of the truth about ourselves. And, behind that, there is the unconscious belief in what we've been talking about. Ignorance and denial are the incubators for all acts such as these. Unworthiness, and the beliefs that grow from it, are like termites in the timber of humanity's house. Sooner or later the structure will become totally undermined and demolition will be inevitable. Sometimes, if structural damage is too severe, it is easier to build a new house than repair the old one.

My analogy of humanity's situation being like a house undermined by termites is not a prediction for the end of the world. But who knows? It seems that we do need a new structure. In truth, the end of the world does comes to each of us at some point in our life. At least the world we had known. Oftentimes when we accept a different way of seeing things our world changes. It may even end. Couples split, careers end, people die. Any of these is the ending of a world, the world we occupied for however long those situations kept it intact. Facing the end of anything is difficult, even when it's things we may say we're tired of, don't like, or maybe even hate. We might hate them, but at least we know them. They're familiar. What's that old saying? the devil you know is better than the one you don't? I guess it's kind of like that. Change can be scary. Change can be hard. Change can be challenging. But—and this is key—change is inevitable. Nothing is static. Our resistance only adds to our pain, and our pain adds to our fear. But there is good news! Add enough pain and there begins to develop a willingness. We begin to finally wake up to the fact that things aren't working. A very significant change is starting to happen right now as you are reading this book.

There is a growing awareness and agreement that we need to change the path humanity has been traveling. There is a spiritual hunger being sensed on a global scale in a way that's not happened before. This has been helped along by technology and communication. For the first time as a species we are able to communicate instantly from anywhere on the planet. This is no accident. As events unfold around the globe we all know about it. Witness the mass global demonstrations that were orchestrated to take place simultaneously as a protest during the weeks leading up to the U.S. invasion of Iraq. Many of us are finally questioning the old ways of doing things—and we're able to share this knowledge. This change is manifesting through people seeking answers and solutions to what is no longer working in their lives or in their world.

But this has also caused many to react in fear. The rise in Fundamentalism is symptomatic of this fear. Fundamentalism thrives on a desire to go back rather than forward. In times of change and instability "that old time religion" seems attractive, safe and comforting. But it is none of those things. What it is instead is a further reinforcement of this age old mistaken message, the very root cause of so much suffering in our world: unworthiness. Whether it is Islamic, Christian, Judaic, or some other form of fundamentalism, doesn't matter. Fundamentalism relies on fear to attract, and more importantly, to keep followers in line: fear of punishment and damnation; fear of separation from God; fear that we are not good enough or holy enough unless we do as we're told by those who know what God wants. Fundamentalism says it offers the only way to eternal salvation and without it we are doomed. Well, the truth is that without a belief in unworthiness and separation, fundamentalism is doomed. Learning about and accepting your true nature is not in their best interest. But obviously it is in yours.

Believe it or not, the high incidence of addictions, as well as the extreme materialism in western culture, are further evidence of this change I'm speaking of here. I know: those things would seem to suggest just the opposite—further evidence of moral decline and a world lost to itself. On the surface that does seem a logical conclusion. But if you look closer you see something quite different: awareness that something is missing. That is a very big step forward! People sense that something is needed. They're just settling for a poor substitute. But—and here is the good news in this—at least they are *realizing* something *is* missing! People are trying to fill the void they feel. In truth it is not a void, it simply feels that way. But it is stillness calling, and the way to that stillness is through emptiness, and that can feel very frightening. Especially in a society like ours where we are taught to believe that practically all our answers involve doing or getting something.

I'm going to venture a guess that all of us, if we're really honest with ourselves, are feeling this calling. We know something is changing, we're just not sure what it is changing to. But we feel "it" deeply. And this causes many of us to feel uneasy and fearful. That's why the increase in fundamental religious beliefs has had such a resurgence. But what is beginning to happen is actually a very good thing. It's evolutionary, it's time to wake up. Humanity is on the threshold of a leap forward.

What is calling to us all is what we came into this life with. Think of it as a seed—a divine seed. And it is ready to take root. Just as a plant instinctively reaches and turns toward the sun, we too seek our Source. Each human being born on this earth is born with this desire to know and experience God, because in this experiencing we will know our true Self. We will be "home". We are all called, and this hunger is completely natural. However, when we ignore it we suffer. Not because we are being punished, but because we resist our true nature. It's painful and difficult trying to be what you are not! That's why so many of us have been trying to "fix" ourselves. Often the solutions we seek, whether it be to heal our sense of unworthiness, or to satisfy this spiritual yearning, are the same. And so are the results. But sometimes the only thing that wakes us up is the unbearable pain of our life falling apart. For some this has been the price that had to be paid. That certainly was the case with me. But will our world wake up in time to prevent disaster and unbearable pain? Are we doomed?

You can never be doomed! Perhaps suffer needlessly, but never without benefit. There is no "doom". The question you have heard in your own mind is the correct one: would you yourself have been willing to change without the pain? Would you have started to wake up without the "tragedy" as you saw it?

The explanation here is that we will never be doomed because we don't end. Our human experience may end. As a matter of fact, it most certainly will end for each of us. And it may even end for humanity as a whole. But, and this is key, we will not end. That is why there is no such thing as doom for us. But I also draw your attention to the words "suffer needlessly". I have no desire to do that, and I'll bet you don't either. Until and unless we accept that we are totally loved, accepted, AND worthy, we will never be at peace. There will always be a missing piece (and peace) for us. We will continue to believe the answer, or solution, is "out there" and always just beyond our grasp.

For those who are seeking spirituality, a relationship with the Divine and their higher Self, and looking for answers through teachers, religious community and fellowship, there is one caution I bring you. While there are great teachers and teachings available, and many wonderful spiritual texts as well, we should not be seduced or get lost in any of these. The danger is this: when we become enthralled with a person, a teacher or a teaching, or even an institution itself, we may mistake them for what we seek. We come to see them as THE WAY, or our solution. This is not unlike the other "solutions" many have tried to use, and the results may be every bit as painful in the end. Witness cults such as The Heavens Gate. Or once again, some of the charismatic fundamentalist leaders. We should never relinquish our power to anyone but God, and for that we need no one to intercede on our behalf. Unfortunately far too many of us are willing—even anxious—to believe that the power is in or through someone or something else. This has made the ground fertile for abuse by people with anything but divine intentions, as well as people who may mean well, but are not well.

We're all like Dorothy in the Wizard of Oz, who, after slaying the wicked witch and returning with her broom, thus proving herself worthy of the great, all-knowing Oz's help, found out she already had what she needed all along—and so did the scarecrow, lion and tin man. No one had to give them what they already possessed! The wizard was merely a person like Dorothy, only he had convinced others differently. But it was all done with smoke and mirrors. The power had always been with Dorothy. So, just like Dorothy, you have everything you need to become whatever you choose to be right now, right here, right at this very moment. And when you accept your true nature, you finally begin to realize there is no place like home. And you are there!

Food for Thought

Think of how the world might look if people no longer needed to prove to themselves and everyone else that they were worthy; if they no longer spent so much time trying to uphold their own importance. It's hard to imagine, but try. What do you think life would be like if each of us didn't feel that need to be right all the time? Or to be constantly recognized in order that we might feel valued? What if we no longer had anything to prove—to others, and most importantly, to ourselves? Feeling worthwhile and valued is a key ingredient when people are asked about satisfaction either at home or on the job. We all want to be valued, and too many of us don't feel as if we are, often with very good reason—we're not. But if you accept that you are worthy and totally loved, and believe this to your core, you'll find you have no need to look to others to confirm this. You'll know, and once you know, well, you know! It's that simple. Understanding this really changes everything: how you relate to yourself, how you treat yourself, and ultimately how you treat others. Because this fact is true for you and of you, it is also true of everyone else you meet, regardless of whether they know it or not. But once you know this, you're going to want to let them know it too. It's amazing how this changes your perspective, and how others react to you as you change how you act toward them. Accepting you are worthy is the solution! It is the beginning of a much happier existence, for you and all concerned. Once you get it, others get it, and like a pebble dropped in a still pond, the ripples travel out and out until they reach the edge of the pond itself.

3

Love or Separation: You Decide

You are totally loved, no matter what. There is nothing you need to do in order to earn this love. There are absolutely no strings attached. No matter what you do, that love will never be withdrawn. You are loved in every aspect, every part, every situation, every moment, always and all ways, completely and absolutely. There has never been a time when it hasn't been so, no matter how things may have looked to you at a given moment.

In the last chapter I said that each of us comes to this life with a desire to know our Source. Well, this is the nature of our Source, and it's closer than the next breath you'll take. You see: you are a perfect design, despite what you may have thought. Nothing can or will ever deprive you of this love. It would be like expecting the sun to suddenly withdraw its light. This is not possible,because it is the sun's nature to produce light. As long as the sun is there, the light is there. Love is the nature of God. As long as God is here, the love is here. And there is no place that God is not. God will never not be here.

So, what do I mean when I say that you decide? Well, as I said in the last chapter, your life is up to you. You do get to chose what to think, where to direct those thoughts, and what to accept or believe. This Divine love is always available to you. All you need do to engage it is to recognize it. In other words: say it is so and it will be so. Does this mean that if you say it isn't so then there will be no love for you? No. The love will still be there. If you closed your eyes would it mean that the sun was gone? You'd simply be depriving yourself of its light. It's the same thing here. You get to decide whether or not to open your eyes. Now here's the thing about love: unlike all other things in the material world, it is inexhaustible. As a matter of fact, it's the one thing that, the more you give away, the more you have. This is Divine nature: inexhaustible, and often paradoxical. But what does this *really mean* to you personally? Well, for starters it means that you've been living your life from illusion if you've believed anything other than this truth. And this truth brings you to the ultimate truth:

There is no part of you that is not part of God. God is in every cell and atom of your being. You are made of what God is. God is the Source and you are the effect of that Source.

I know: old beliefs can be very hard to get past. I followed along reading each word as my hand wrote this message. My immediate reaction was disbelief. After all, if God was always right with me and in all parts of me, then why didn't I feel it? and why did I sometimes have such pain in my life? And what about all the other people in the world? If God was there, then how and why did so many bad things happen? Where was God at Auschwitz and all the other killing fields? Here's what I was told:

God was there because God is always there. God was with the person going to the gas chamber, and the guard escorting them there, because it simply can be no other way.

This answer troubled me. It went against practically all I had once believed. This, even though I thought I no longer believed those things! The emotion it evoked was powerful. It said: no way! It said: that makes no sense! How can it be??! It seemed to diminish God, make Him like one of us and powerless to change anything. Who wants a

God like that? Not me. Give me the all-powerful version, the one who intervenes and saves people. But wait a minute! Isn't that the one I had all the trouble with years earlier? The superhero version of God who dons his cape and flies in to save the day…sometimes…maybe…or not.

So although this answer troubled me, it also relieved me. But just the same, being told that God was with all those people throughout history and horror didn't comfort me a whole lot. After all, they still died, didn't they? And it certainly hadn't been an easy death for many of them. The enormity of such things was just too big for me to really fathom. I needed to put this in a more understandable perspective, to reduce it down to something manageable. That led me to the thing I am usually led to when trying to understand anything. The only point of reference I *really* know: me. After all, I had no way of knowing what those people experienced. But I did know what I experienced during some of the darkest times in my own life. And so, although the comparison really paled alongside such terrible things, it was all I had. I asked from a personal perspective: Where was God all those times I was alone and lonely? Those times when I suffered and was scared?

With you, experiencing what you experienced

With that answer a door opened for me! And it has opened wider and wider with the passage of time and my deepening understanding of what was told to me that day. Not only had God known what was going on for me, including what I was feeling. God had experienced what I'd experienced, felt every tug at my heart, every disappointment, every hurt and humiliation, all the fear and anger. Whatever it had been, God had been there. But it would be almost 2 years after receiving this answer before I would begin to understand what it really said! And in that understanding it started to make sense to me! The difference between us was in God's understanding of the experience! In other words: *God did and I didn't.*

When things happen, there are reasons that may be (and usually are) outside our understanding at the time. Remember this: we see only a very, very tiny segment of what truly is. Or as has often been said, through a glass darkly. How could anyone be expected to know what is best with that kind of perspective? Furthermore, most of us have been conducting our life from that perspective. And let's not forget the mistaken beliefs we've been carrying around regarding our worthiness. No wonder things have been so hard!

But what about all the cruelty and horrors in this world? How does knowing that God has been there help us to accept these things—to tolerate such things? Well, first let me point out that acceptance does not equal approval. We needn't approve of anything. But if we continually fight against what is or what was, rehashing it over and over again, we place our self in a state of perpetual struggle and turmoil. This is not a state of consciousness that helps anyone or anything. It does not serve our higher purpose. On the contrary. It traps us in a feedback loop, negative thought and fear feeding negative thought and fear. We stay angry, we stay resentful, we stay scared. And in this we reinforce and give strength to that which we don't want. And our awareness stays trapped in the things that aren't real. You may be saying to yourself, what do you mean, "not real"? Just look around and see the mess! That's as real as the nose on my face. Well, yes it is—and every bit as temporary, too! Neither will last. This is something I will return to several times throughout this book. We often believe the temporary is real and dismiss the eternal. Talk about having things backwards!

Okay, so then how do we heal all of this? How do we stop more of it from happening? And probably most important of all, how do we forgive it? Believe it or not, the answer to the first two questions is found in the third question: forgive. But how is that possible after such terrible things? First we must remember: we only do these things again and again because we have denied our connection to God, and through that connection, to each other. How could any of us really harm another if we knew *who* it was we harmed? Jesus told us this when he said that whatever we do to the least one of us we also do to him. We are all connected, each and every one of us—from the lowest among us to the mightiest, most powerful politician or leader on earth. We, each and every one of us, are all a part of the same Thing. But we've believed the illusion we've created. We believed it so strongly that it now is our reality. This is the house built on sand that Christ spoke of. We've built an intricate and involved structure, imagining we were on rock, but we've been wrong! And we've been told this time and again over the centuries. Hundreds of years before Christ, prophets and spiritual teachers had been telling us of our illusion of separateness. By the time of Jesus we'd already been believing in our separateness for thousands of years. Despite all that he told us, we heard practically none of it!

What we did manage to hear was filtered through centuries of misunderstanding. And what little we heard called on us to change our ways radically! We were told to love one another; to forgive and then forgive even more; to turn the other cheek, to love our enemies and wish them well, to bless those who curse and persecute us!

Almost any change is difficult for us. But something like this? It seemed impossible. We are creatures of habit, even when the habits aren't very healthy. We tend to stay with what we know, even if we're miserable doing it. Change is something that rarely happens by our own choice, unless something happens to force us. Well, it's time we opened our eyes because something is definitely happening. An alcoholic or drug addict doesn't seek help because his life is working. It takes the loss of practically everything before he finally becomes willing to change and try a different way. The rest of humanity is not much different.

One definition of insanity is doing the same thing over and over again, but expecting different results. That description describes what's been happening here on Earth for the past six thousand years or so. Despite all our advancements we still conduct ourselves in very much the same way as we always have: threats, force, retaliation, domination, blackmail and coercion, intrigue and dishonesty, subversion and oppression. We have made some progress. But unfortunately it seems that our technology has made a good deal more progress than we have! We have much catching up to do in order to get through this time in which we are currently living. I asked about this.

The world will be transformed one person at a time. There will come a point when this momentum will be unstoppable. A critical mass will be reached. Not every person on the planet must come to this realization in order for it to come about.

So, like a tide that raises all ships, there will come a point when all of us will be raised. *What* that critical number is, I have no idea, only that once we hit a certain point it would be unstoppable. It would become exponential.

The late visionary, Buckminster Fuller, coined the term "space ship Earth". He said that we're all on it together, with no way off, so we'd better take care of it and learn to cooperate and get along. Well, the message is that our space ship will change course as soon as enough of us change our internal course. So, whether the number of people needed to accomplish this course correction is a billion, or only a hundred thousand of us, the truth is this: it begins with you. It begins in your heart. What you cultivate there affects the world. That's why I'm here giving you this message. You may be the one who tips the balance.

Anything and everything you have done that has harmed you or another has been done in ignorance of the truth of Who you are. This is not an excuse. It does not relieve you of responsibility for your actions. However, compassion is absolutely essential while accepting that responsibility. With that compassion comes the key ingredient: forgiveness. Forgive yourself and all others as well. Remember: they have been in that same boat with you, and even if they're still asleep to this change taking place on our planet, you no longer are. Forgiveness is one of the most healing and transformative things you can ever do. And, most importantly, it allows you to make things right through changing your actions and the way you live.

As you've been told, each and every one of us arrived here in this life "knowing" that we're worthy, loved and connected. But then we developed a sort of "collective amnesia" around this knowledge. This forgetting got helped along by the things we all were taught and told as we begin to mature. This knowledge gets "trained" out of us. The more we buy into the smaller reality the less we see of the greater reality. And we fall ever deeper into forgetting. Had we remembered our connection to God and each other, we never would have succumbed to the myths of separation and unworthiness. Had we remembered, there would have been no one to commit the terrible atrocities that history is littered with, and there'd be no one continuing the tradition today. There would have been no reason for them. Why would we do that to our self? We are all part of the very same thing. We are unique aspects and experiences of the One that is God. Your amnesia is over if you choose it to be.

4

REAL POWER MEANS REAL RESPONSIBILITY.

Nelson Mandela said: "Our deepest fear is not that we are inadequate, but rather that we are powerful beyond measure." Mr. Mandela was definitely on to something here. Because the truth is that we are exactly that! What's that you're saying? Show me the power…?? Well when you've been looking at the wrong things to measure it, and then feeding a mistaken belief with continually reinforcing thoughts and actions, it could be staring you in the face and you'd never even know it. That's exactly what you've been doing. Don't worry, you're not alone. You have loads of company.

Here's one of the things that trips us up: we mistake what real power is in this world. We see material manifestations of things we believe represent power. Things like money, fame, social standing, job, connections, physical prowess. We conclude that they represent what real power is. But think about that for a moment. How powerful is something that is so transitory, so ephemeral? It is only powerful in a very tiny realm of what this universe is. And—even more importantly—only for an extremely short period of time. This applies to an individual or a nation. A nation may be the preeminent world power for five centuries—maybe even a thousand years—but how long is that when compared to the time that the earth has been in existence? A family may exercise great power through wealth and influence for generations. Again I ask, how long is that?

When viewed from the perspective of a child or teenager, our life appears as if it will go on indefinitely. But as we approach our middle years, this view begins to change drastically. Suddenly we're asking ourselves how we got there. What happened to all the time we thought we had? Days, weeks, months, and finally years fly by. Just yesterday the kids were playing in the yard, or fighting over the TV. Suddenly the house is quiet and there are no more squabbles or feet flying up the stairs, no small jackets left tossed on chairs. Where did it all go so fast? Visit a nursing home and ask a resident how long ago it was that they were a child. They will most likely tell you it feels as if it were yesterday. Everything is relative. And everything we see before us passes away.

When we live our life from the perspective of things such as jobs, possessions, money or connections granting us power, we are at the mercy of those things. They are our master. Yet they are poor masters. We've given power to things that will eventually be impossible to hold on to. They will fade away or fail us. Spend time with the person who is at the end of his life and ask him what matters to them. You'll never hear someone say that they wish they'd spent more time at the office. But unfortunately, for far too many of us, perspective only comes at the end, if at all. Does this mean that we shouldn't hold things like career and finances important? No. It means we should see them for what they are. And in that seeing, their importance in our lives will be reduced to scale.

Okay, if what constitutes real power isn't any of these things, then what is it? And why on earth would we fear being more powerful than we imagined??? Let me answer the second part of that question first. We fear it because, if the power is really in our hands, it means we are responsible. As you've been told, you are the effect of the Source most of us call God and nothing can ever separate you from God. That means you are always connected, and that gives you access to the Power of your Source. How? Through your thoughts, imaginings, intentions, and beliefs. That's why it's so important to set this worthiness thing right. You see: *we are what we think*. It's that simple! Jesus said: "As a man thinketh, so is he". The Buddha said we become what our thoughts make us. Here is the truth behind those statements: Our thoughts connect us to our Source and our Source returns in kind what those thoughts instruct. Does that mean you are able to materialize what you think about? Yes. But for most of us, this is usually a long and drawn out process. It's cumulative, and we don't see it because it often takes years, even decades. Bit by bit, what our mind cultivates comes to us in one way or another. But, because this process is so slow, we often don't see what it is that's happening. We choose to believe our life is the result of random and external events, or things like luck, and that we are at the mercy of life and what it hands us. This is another myth we need to discard. You see, as long as we believe it, then it is so! That is the meaning of the quote from Nelson Mandela. Although he was in prison for years, he was never imprisoned. He knew they couldn't take what was rightfully his, no matter how long they kept him locked away. And with his certainty in the truth he knew about himself, he rose to become a world leader and the first Black president of the very nation whose prison could not break him.

Thoughts are things. Powerful things! Consider this: practically everything you currently use in your life was once merely a thought, an idea someone had. Whether its the TV you watch, the car you drive, the stove you cook with, the house you live in, all of these stemmed from a thought had by a person or group of people. Okay, it's easy to see that inventions and devices had to be thought of first. Common sense would certainly back up the need for a set of blueprints before starting construction of a house, and obviously somebody had to draw them up. The design had to originate somewhere. But this is also the way events, circumstances, and situations take form and shape. This is how our very lives unfold.

In the past quarter century, medical science has accepted that there is a mind-body connection, even though this idea was initially scoffed at and dismissed as nonsense. How we think most definitely affects our physical health. Today quantum physics is showing us a very different view of so-called reality. In many ways it is turning the world that we believed existed on its ear. Things previously thought impossible are turning out to be true. Among them the fact that consciousness and matter are linked. It's been proven that the mere act of observation can actually change how a particle reacts, and therefore affect matter itself. It now appears that a particle can actually be in two places at the same time. With each new discovery quantum physics reveals to us, it is becoming ever more evident that science and spirituality are not necessarily at odds. These days they are looking more and more like the same thing seen from different angles. [1]

Anyway, I don't want to get too far off track here. Let's get back to your mind and your thoughts. I'm going to suggest a little exercise here. Close this book and sit still for a few minutes. Take a few deep breaths. Now, begin to look back over your life. Take as much time as you'd like. Make it a life review. Where are you today, and how did you get there? Look back. Remember. What were the things you believed or decided to believe? Was it what others told you? What mattered to you? What matters today? Are they the same? Similar? If not, how have they changed? And why? How about the people in your life? What type of

---

1. At the back of the book I've included a list of books I've found helpful while trying to wrap my mind around these concepts. These books are written for the lay person not the scientist, hence my ability to understand them

things do you like to surround yourself with today? How have they changed since your childhood? Be patient as you do this. I suggest you do this a number of times, because each time will be different, because each time *you* will be different. There is an old saying: we never step into the same river twice. Take time to simply sit and be. Let thoughts come up as you ask yourself these questions. Let me suggest one more question you might want to ask yourself: have I made the whole thing up? Is it real or not? As you ask this and then review, you may notice striking similarities between situations and circumstance in your life. It may appear as if they are variations on each other, or combinations of the same elements arranged in slightly different ways. People you meet today remind you of others you've known. Certain places contain similar aspects or "feels" to other places from your childhood. Consider this: Maybe there are just so many pieces you have to work with as you imagine your life! Or perhaps you just enjoy using certain designs and themes. I'm not telling you that this is so. But then again I am not saying it isn't true either. No matter what you might believe, this can be a very revealing exercise, and a good way to pay attention to things in your life.

Now, I have no way of knowing what your present life circumstances are. It's very possible that things aren't as you'd like them to be. Your life might seem as if it's had a lot of troubles and hard luck. It may seem as if it's really been unfair. And that may be true for a good part of it. But (and this may be a bitter pill to swallow for you) you have had much to do with how things have turned out. This is a good news/bad news scenario. The bad news is that you are responsible for the way things are. And the good news is: no matter what you've thought, you can change what you think—and that means you can change your life. You are part creator, in conjunction or partnership with *The* Creator. You can create, or more correctly, re-create your life. Starting right here, starting right now! That's an amazing thing to know, and now you know it. Henry Ford had said: "if you think you can or you think you can't, you're right!" It is all about what you think.

But there's one thing I'd like to discuss before going any further regarding illness and disease. Disease happens for many reasons. Certainly some life choices can, and do, influence our body and its health. And of course there is the mind-body connection that science now agrees exists. But I take strong issue with any implication that you've "failed" or are not evolved spiritually because you've gotten sick. This seems to be a belief among some "new agers." But I'd like to point out that some of the most spiritually "fit" and evolved people of the 20th century, Jiddu Krishanmurti for example, have died of diseases like cancer. Eventually we all do die of something. The truth is this: often a disease is actually Grace unrecognized. I lost my younger brother to cancer when he was only 9 years old. I don't for a minute believe he brought it on himself through anything like unresolved issues, punishment, or lack of spiritual fitness. I do believe that he made a choice before he came into this life. He chose to be our teacher, and his illness helped and affected others: school mates, parents, and only God knows who else. As terrible as it was for my family to go through the 14 months of Jimmy's illness, and as awful as it was for my parents to lose their youngest child to cancer, the Grace that entered our family and so many other lives through Jim's being here has spread out like a ripple, affecting more lives than I'll ever know. But I do know what it brought to our family, and, while it might have been terrible Grace, it was Grace—and it still is. And the thing about Grace is that its effect moves ever outward, encompassing more and more people as it does. Compassion and empathy, tolerance and forgiveness—these have been some of the fruits of that Grace that first appeared back in 1963. Of course, we didn't see any of this at that time. To us it was a family tragedy. We had no way of knowing what future benefits would be realized. But because we did not see that at the time does not change what it was. Grace is often a matter of perspective.

Returning to the power of your thoughts, here's some unsettling news that you need to be aware of: what you fear and obsess over, you give strength to, and may actually attract. Knowing this fact won't help you. It's more likely to make matters worse. Why? Because once you accept that this is true, you will try your best to get rid of these fears and negative thoughts. That may sound like you're going in the right direction, but here we are again at another paradox. What happens when you "try" to do anything? You focus on it, you become increasingly aware of it. So, although your wish is to be rid of whatever it is, you wind up reinforcing it instead. You work at pushing these things out of your mind. But rather than going out they go down, deeper into the unconscious. But, as you know, just because it's buried doesn't mean it isn't impacting your life.

Okay, so if trying to get rid of negative thinking and fears doesn't really work, then what's a person to do? How *do you avoid this*? The answer may seem counterintuitive: simply let them go. That's right—just let them go. Don't *try* to make them go away. That's like trying to *not* think about a pink rabbit. What happens? You see my point.

Man oh man, this is a hard concept to get! At least it was (and at times, still is) for me. But, by simply *becoming willing* to let go, something happens, slowly but surely. Ask God to take it from you, at God's own convenience. Trust God's timing. Spirit *always* knows the right time. Then trust with your whole heart that the matter has been dealt with. It's no longer your concern. If it's hard for you to really trust, then *pretend* you trust. It's called "acting as if," and it is a powerful tool. With applied practice, it works. If the troubling thought resurfaces (and it almost certainly will) repeat this. Each time, acknowledge that God knows when the time is right for it to be totally gone. Then believe it is so. That's it! Repeat again as needed. Eventually it will be a non-issue. It will simply no longer exist to you.

Now, let's talk about changing your habits of thought. Negative thinking is a habitual way of thinking. It's a learned behavior and response. You've developed these habits over your whole lifetime. But anything that's been learned can be un-learned. Consider this more of the "faulty programming" that's been given to you. If your life today is not as you wish it to be, then this is where you must begin. By accepting your worthiness and reminding yourself frequently of its truth, your other thought patterns begin to be influenced.

However, this fact alone will not prevent the return of negative thinking. As any gardener can tell you, simply planting the best seeds is no guarantee of a good garden. Even if you've painstakingly removed every weed before you planted, new ones will spring up overnight. Without consistent maintenance, they will strangle out what you've planted, and before too long you'll have a garden full of weeds. So it is with your mind. You must pay attention to what you allow to grow there. This is your choice. Become conscious of what you allow into your mind. Maintaining an open mind is vital for expanding one's own horizons and life. But being open does not mean you must allow any sort of riff-raff that happens by to move in. Exposing yourself repeatedly to forms of entertainment that promote violence and negativity, or a steady stream of news (which is so often tilted toward the sensational, negative, and fearful), are things you have control over. You do not need to put your head in the sand, but you also don't need to go swimming in a cesspool. Allow your mind to be exposed to new things, positive things. Listen to music, expose yourself to art, take in the beauty around you, the outdoors and nature. Get a steady diet of these things and you will benefit. This will help you balance the difficult events that do happen in every life. It is food for the soul. Also: start to pay attention to how you talk to others. It's pretty common for most of us to make small talk and this talk is usually laced with complaints, or gossip, or bad news. We don't have to do this. It's all about being conscious, and when we're conscious we get to choose. This is not an easy path, but it is much easier than the one most of us have been on. While it takes work to be conscious, I believe it takes even more work to be unconscious! And the pay-off doesn't compare. Not even close!

Remember: nothing has power over us unless we grant it power. That is how Nelson Mandela could emerge unbroken from an experience that has broken other men. He knew that the power being exerted over him only operated in the physical realm—the material world. He saw that world for what it always is: temporary. In recognizing this, he granted himself the power of choice as to where he would draw his power from. We all have this choice. What will you choose today? It is up to you. Really.

5

The Truth About Pain, Suffering, and Truth

o o o o o o o o o o o o o o o o o o o o o o o o o o o o o o o o
"He who learns must suffer. And even in our sleep pain that cannot forget, falls drop by drop upon the heart, and in our own despair, against our will, comes wisdom to us by the awful grace of God."

—*Aeschylus*

If you were hoping I was going to give you the answer to eliminating pain and struggle in your life, I have some bad news for you. The truth is: as long as you are here in this life you will continue to experience these things. What can be accomplished is a reduction in the incidences, and the development of an ability to transcend them. Life is not intended to be too comfortable or easy. But why is it that things can be <u>so</u> hard for some of us? Why does life seem such a struggle at times? I'm reminded of a scene from a movie. One night as I was flipping around the TV dial, I stumbled upon an old movie. I'm always a sucker for these black and white windows into the America we had once believed (hoped) existed. So I began watching. This particular scene was in a baseball stadium, after the game. A kid who quite obviously idolized this bunch of ball players was waiting in line to get an autograph. When it was his turn, as he handed his baseball to one of his heroes, he asks him a simple question: why is it so hard to "get good" at baseball? The ballplayer looks down at the boy, grins and winks as he says: "kid, being hard is what makes it great!"

Obviously, being 'hard' is what keeps so many from even attempting it. The few who do, and stick with it, are the ones who might make it to the pros. That's the price they are willing to pay, and that's what this ballplayer was telling that boy. The same thing applies to just about everything in life. And that is what I began thinking about as I started this chapter: the price we pay for the lessons we learn. Or fail to learn. Either way we pay; the only matter up for grabs is how, and with what. But isn't there a little bit of the bargain hunter in all of us? Isn't there a special appeal in paying half-price? Better yet, something for nothing is practically irresistible. Isn't that what we are doing when we try to circumvent the work needed to gain what it is we want? The easy way is deliciously appealing, isn't it? When we seem to succeed, finding what we believe is a short-cut, don't we all feel like we put something over on someone? Got away with it? Avoided the pain and got all the gain? Lottery ticket sales depend on this desire. So do casinos and games of "chance". So do all the sales advertising "no payments until January in the year 2010 if you'll only buy today!" And interest will be deferred as well! What a deal! You get to enjoy something like a car, big screen TV, or dining room set for months, maybe even years, before any bill appears. But rest assured, that bill will come. Often by the time you begin to pay for whatever it is you bought, the thing has already lost its luster. It's no longer new. It might even be broken. Doesn't matter. You agreed and now its time to pay up. There is no such thing as something-for-nothing

Often in our life and our experiences, because payment has been deferred to a later date, we have little idea what the final tab will come to. Unbeknownst to us, interest adds up quickly. Sometimes we never realize the things that have been included in the bill we've unwittingly paid. This is the <u>real</u> cost to us. *Real* cost can be measured in many ways: Failed relationships, heartache, missed opportunities, paths not taken, careers not pursued, poor decisions, illness and disease, physical injury, to name only a few. The odds that we will learn, and then value it enough to remember what we've learned, seem much more likely when we've paid, either out of pocket, body or heart. Too often if we are simply given something, and we've put none of ourselves into it (i.e. toil, sweat, tears, saving, working, planning) we don't value it. We often lose interest quickly and take it for granted. This seems to be a part of human nature. And for many of us this also applies to the natural gifts and abilities we came into this world with (more on this subject a little later in the book).

Practically all of us know of someone, or maybe we've even <u>been</u> that someone, who has always been given everything and never been required to work for it. The kid who has every toy imaginable, yet seems bored. The 16 year old who is given the brand new car of his or her choosing as soon as he gets his license. The young adult who has his own apartment, yet mom and dad pay the rent. The word we use to describe them is "spoiled," which may be followed by the word "rotten." Interestingly, if either of these words is applied to our food, we don't eat it! In these examples I've given you, the person has been deprived of the experience of working to accomplish something, and deprived of learning that they themself are capable. They, in turn, do not value the things they get. Why should they? They have nothing of themselves invested in it. But even more damaging, they don't value themselves. The message they've received is, "You can't—so we will".

I'd like to tell you a personal story. But it's not the story I had intended to tell when I'd started this chapter. That version currently lies in the paper bin by my desk, ready to go out with the recycling. And, by the way, the things I discovered while writing it are on their way to a different kind of trash bin. But not before I share the lesson with you.

When I was 15, I really wanted a new guitar amplifier. *Needed* it, is the way I put it. The amp I had tended to blow fuses when it got hot. But just as importantly, it didn't look very good. In the world of rock and roll image is everything, and size definitely does matter! My band was working regularly, playing beach club dances weekly. I began saving some of the money I was earning. I wanted that new, "bigger" amplifier as soon as possible. One night, my amplifier blew one too many fuses, and I decided I just had to get the new one right away. But I hadn't saved enough money. So I hit my mom up for a loan to cover the gap between what I had and what I needed. It came to about $200—a lot of money in 1968, especially to a teenager. Mom agreed to advance me the money—provided I make a payment after each gig until I paid the balance off. In my enthusiasm, I even offered to give her half of whatever I made in order to show the sincerity I had for making good on the loan. The deal was struck, and I got the new amplifier. For a while all was well. It was big, it looked good, and it sounded great! I gladly handed over half my pay after each gig, my Mom recording these payments in a small spiral note book.

But as the weeks went by I began to be interested in spending some of that money on other things I now "needed". Plus (and this was the big one) I'd finally gotten a girlfriend! I figured that the new amp probably had something to do with that. Anyway, I needed money to take her out to the movies and such. Surely my mom would understand that. Well, when I tried to renegotiate our terms she seemed to have little sympathy for my new circumstances. Girlfriend or no girlfriend, we had made a deal. And, as she was quick to point out to me, she wasn't taking all my pay, only half. That meant I still had money to take my girl out, just not all the time. I'd have to "budget" myself. I didn't like that word.

So I tried a different tactic. I forgot to give her the money one night after I'd returned from playing. I didn't say anything the next day and neither did she. I'd gotten away with it! Or so I thought. But the next time I played she was waiting for me when I got home. There was no getting past her. I gave her half of what I'd made that night. She then asked me for my missed payment. I was so angry that I took the money, every bit I'd made that night (which was about $25 in one dollar bills) and tossed it across the kitchen table where she sat. I said something to the effect of "if you need the money so bad, then here, have it!!!". Truthfully I was hoping she'd feel sorry for me, when she saw how upset I was. Maybe she'd even give some of the money back to me. Well she didn't, at least not that night. But what did happen was that she began to ease up on her requests for payments. If she did ask, I began crying the blues, saying I hardly made any money and that I never had any cash to do anything. As time went on my Mom seemed to lose any stomach for these exchanges. Finally she stopped asking altogether, and I never, ever offered.

My original intention had been to use this story to illustrate how we value what we work and pay for. I wanted to give a personal perspective. But, obviously I can't. That's the version presently waiting to go curbside. When I began writing that story, I had "forgotten" the fact that I never finished paying for that amplifier! That part of the story just didn't jibe with the person I want to believe myself to be! You see, when my 17th birthday had arrived, Mom had handed me the book, marked paid in full. She'd written off the balance I still owed, giving it as a birthday present.

I have told the story of my mom and her payment book to my own kids as an example of how I learned to budget and be responsible; wearing it like a badge of honor and proof positive that I'd not been a spoiled kid. But I'd been telling a revised version of the story. Yet I didn't know it. I believed this was the real story. It's funny, but when you alter something, and tell it enough times, that's what becomes "real" to you. Or so you think. The actual story had never *really* gone away. It just lay buried. But apparently I did "feel" about it. And that was a problem—one I didn't realize was there. What we conceal does not heal or go away! Another discovery I made when I uncovered this truth was the fact that I had a tendency to hold back information—to not tell the whole story, but rather my own edited version. I had never viewed myself as a secretive person, yet this is what I came to realize. It seemed I had a much stronger fear of criticism and ridicule than I'd ever imagined. This fear caused me to be selective as to what I was willing to share about myself with others, even those closest to me.

So, returning to the story of the amplifier: the lesson I initially learned was not the one my mother had intended to teach me when we'd first set out on this deal. But today I do know that *I did* pay for that amplifier. But the cost was much more dear than the dollars I was so reluctant to part with. It became clear to me that the lesson I took from this influenced many of my actions for years to come. What had I learned? That there were ways around things, that my word wasn't always important, and that I could change the terms to meet any new circumstances that might benefit me more. This way of doing things didn't really sit well with me. As a matter of fact, it went against the values I'd been taught while growing up. Yet I behaved this way over and over again. Why? Because it worked. And there was always a good reason, at least as far as I was concerned. There was always a justification I could use. Rationalization and justification were my biggest allies. I came to rely on them. When we find something that seems to serve us, we use it. It worked, and I learned to work it. Not always, but certainly enough. And as I grew older, I continued this behavior. That's what I learned as I wrote this. I've been hiding this truth about myself from myself for years. And as I continued to write, the plot thickened, and I began to see even more.

I now not only see, but understand, how this has affected the way I've felt about myself, and it's led me to see other things from my past that I was totally unaware of. It explains my uneasiness sometimes when being questioned, feeling as if the person asking is trying to catch me in an inconsistency or lie, causing a defensiveness that's been very uncomfortable for me. I've often wondered why I had these feelings. They rarely corresponded to the situation, yet the feelings were real. At the beginning of this book, I mentioned that I failed to confide in Jane after my experience on that hillside. That is a perfect example of this behavior in action. Of all the people in the world, there is no one I feel more accepted by or approved of than Jane. And I've always believed that I share everything with her. Yet I didn't tell her this. My fear had absolutely no grounding in what was real, yet it informed my behavior.

This contradiction between what I did and what I wished to believe had been at odds for years. No wonder I was uneasy. So this writing process has been very much like digging in the cemetery for me—or maybe it's the dump. Either way, obviously a lot of stuff's been buried for a long time. I'm willing to bet that each one of us has a similar tale buried somewhere.

But there is an answer: *accept and forgive. Accept* the truth of what happened, then *forgive* yourself. Take responsibility, and don't do it again. Discovering your flaws, imperfections, and less than admirable acts is not meant to punish you—it's meant to teach you what not to do! And taking it one step further: when you see your own imperfections and forgive them, you are able to look at others and have compassion when they struggle with theirs.

Looking back and remembering the person I'd once been, I do understand why I felt a need to create this particular story. You see, I lived in a beautiful home and had parents with money, but I never wanted to be considered a "rich kid". To be called that was an insult to me. I did my best to conceal the privilege I came from. Both my folks had come from very modest backgrounds and worked their way up. There was a family myth that had grown out of these humble origins. I wanted my own myth: that I'd always been responsible, somewhat frugal, and that I worked for whatever I'd gotten. All qualities I admired. So I created a story that omitted some of the facts and made me look the way I *wanted* to look.

But in finally coming clean with myself, I have had to face the truth: at times I have been anything but these things I was taught to value. I often behaved irresponsibly, despite telling myself otherwise. I bought things I really couldn't afford. I borrowed money without thinking of how I'd repay it, and I took advantage of my parents' good heart and generosity. That is the truth, and it hurts for me to face it, admit it, and say it out loud. But, I don't behave this way today. That sort of behavior is part of my "pre-1991" repertoire.

The price I paid for this behavior has caused me a great deal of emotional pain, the loss of a business, and a number of financial hardships. Still I remained more or less clueless for years. Not that I couldn't see that things weren't working for me. I just didn't know why. Furthermore, I often believed many of my difficulties were caused by others. My road back has been bumpy. When my life hit the wall in the early 1990's I was devastated—brought to my knees. And that was actually a gift—THE GIFT. Today I know that in the midst of all those terrible things there was Grace washing over me, inundating me. The tragedies unfolding in my life stopped me, and then the Grace carried me. I learned to live by a new set of principles that were really very much in step with the way I'd always *wanted* to be. And my life began to improve by leaps and bounds. I can't emphasize this enough. The way things began working out in my life was truly remarkable—some would even say miraculous. This new way of living felt right to me. It was a path that encouraged rigorous self-honesty, congruency between word and action, and enlarging my spiritual life. This has not been easy, nor has it been a quick-fix, feel-good-right-away solution. It has been a gradual process that I need to continually practice. But the results were apparent to me almost right from the start. I felt clearer and at peace in a way I'd not felt since being a small boy, despite the fact that my life was in such drastic transition.

Yet it still took me 13 years to make the discovery that I've just shared with you. As I said a moment ago, I have not behaved this way in a long time. But apparently the scars created by this behavior had stayed with me. The "feelings", if not the memories, remained active. That's been this uneasy feeling that still returns to me on occasion, the one that says I'm a fraud or a liar, although nothing I am doing corresponds to it. The feeling I get is real, although the situation is not. But thankfully this has not been running my life as it once had, because I do live so differently today. Whenever these feelings come up I remind myself that they have no basis in my present life. This helps. Although I still might fall victim to a dark mood washing over me, I know the mood will pass. And that is a very big difference from the way it used to be for me.

Though totally unintended, my real story of truth and consequences probably does a much better job of making the point I had hoped to make with my original story. It is funny how things work out. This story contains a message for both the kid in us, and the parent we may become or already are. What was done for me with the best of intentions by someone who loved me most in the world did not, in the long run, do what she would have hoped for me. And in truth I have been guilty of the same with my own children. It is always hard to see those you love in pain and struggling. It is only natural that we wish to help. Often, letting them experience the pain and the consequences of the action is the most loving thing we can really do for them. But few of us have the insight or the courage to do that. Who wishes to appear mean or uncaring? And that's what this might look like, even if the opposite is really true. In truth it might be the highest form of love we can give, and maybe the greatest gift. Perhaps this is the way it works between God and us as well.

◆   ◆   ◆

Pain and struggle are teachers. They are not meant to punish us. We determine that. Pain may be the only thing that finally gets us to stop doing what we've been doing. The emotional and spiritual pain I experienced back in 1991 was what it took to finally get me to stop doing the things I'd continually done in my attempts to avoid my pain. They'd stopped working and I had no choice but to turn and face what I'd been feeling. Pain often provides us the opportunity to know ourselves in deeper ways—ways not possible had we not experienced that pain. While the process is not pleasant, the reward almost always overshadows the pain of learning the particular lesson…eventually. Look again at your life. Haven't some of your greatest lessons come out of your most painful experiences?

Take a minute and think about what your life would be like if you had no pain. How would you know if something was wrong? At first you might think that the absence of pain would be a wonderful thing. But if you didn't experience pain what would warn you if you were straining something, either physically, emotionally or spiritually? If you never experienced not feeling well would you really know that you actually felt good when you did? You'd have nothing to compare it to, and feeling good would have no meaning. If you've never felt illness how would you know the condition we call health? Like it or not, pain is not only necessary, but it is often a great gift. But usually the gift isn't something we can see at the time.

I believe one of the great gifts pain and struggle gives to us is perspective. Going through an experience such as illness, financial setback, death of a loved one or friend, we often see things differently. What once seemed *so* important, no longer is. That's a change in perspective. I once spoke with a man who had gone through a complete breakdown, and for a time been a homeless street person in New York City. Having once been a successful professional, he'd fallen as far as one can seemingly fall. But that fall led him to seek help and he eventually recovered. He told me that today practically all his problems are "steak and lobster problems." In one word they are luxuries. The things that had once overwhelmed him and eventually broke him no longer rattled him. His priorities had changed along with his perspective.

Pain occurs on three levels: physical, emotional, and spiritual. It is possible for pain to stay localized to only one realm when it is in the physical. We can have great physical pain, yet emotionally and spiritually we are fine. J. Krishnamurti, one of the great teachers of the twentieth century, was stricken with stomach cancer, a terribly painful form of this disease; yet he made the distinction as to *who* suffered when speaking to his followers: he did not, his body did. Emotionally and spiritually he was fine, yet the body was dying in an agonizing way. Not to dismiss the seriousness of this, because pain such as this can be excruciating. But the fact that spiritually and emotionally he was in health allowed him to move beyond the pain in the physical and not be its prisoner, tortured until the end finally came. So pain may be present in the physical and not at the emotional and spiritual, and if this is the case there is no suffering, only physical pain.

But this is not so when either of these other two realms experience pain. Emotional pain will eventually bleed over into the physical realm and may manifest as physical symptoms. If it goes untreated for too long, it may even become disease. However, the most damaging and destructive pain we will ever experience happens when we become separated from our spirit. This might occur because we've experienced something that we've allowed to cut this umbilical cord—either something external or internal has happened and we've allowed it to lead us to this terrible place. We can overcome all manner of physical hardship and emotional pain through tapping into the strength of the spirit. But if our spiritual connection is severed, then it's as if all hope is gone. This *is* the experience of hell. This deep wounding is despair of the worst kind, and provides fertile ground for self-hatred, addictions, and all of the worst behaviors humanity is capable of. This is suffering!

Is there a way back from this experience? or is it, as the stories of fire and brimstone say, suffering for all eternity—cut off from God? You already have the answer to that, it was given to you in the beginning of this book: nothing can ever separate you from God-except your own perception. The answer then lies within you. All that is required for the connection to be realized again is to make it so. This is done by inviting God back into your life, and if God has never been a part of your life, then this would be the time to change that!

Many a drug addict, alcoholic, murderer, criminal, or desperately sick person has experienced a profound spiritual awakening, and this has been their way out of hell. These people are transformed and those who've known them before and then encountered them after this has happened are often amazed by that transformation. They are not the same person at all! Personally, I believe that the only way out of this situation is through some sort of profound spiritual intervention or awakening. It is possible for any person to experience this, no matter what they've done—no matter how far they may have sunk. But sadly, compared to the large numbers of sufferers, very few do. However the ones who do make it back from this terrible condition carry the message to others, as is witnessed in 12 Step recovery programs and all manner of support groups. It's also seen in the heroic efforts of many survivors of horrific deeds, as they heal from what was believed to be un-healable, by taking this healing out to the world.

So the truth is that spiritual growth is a struggle, and it is often painful, and at times may be close to agony itself. But there is always a reason, and again this begs our trust. After all, if we were just simply given the answers, would they matter to us? Could we even understand them? I remind myself of this when I see things happen in the world. I remind myself of this when I see one of my own kids wrestling with some of the things I once struggled with. Often I try to pass on what I learned through my experience, but most times they say thanks and then keep on doing what they've been doing. That's the way life is. We get it when it's time for us to get it! Not that passing on my experience isn't helpful, because it is. But it is my experience and not theirs.

Sharing my experience is the planting of a seed. The timing of when things are realized and understood isn't up to me. But of course, this doesn't mean I don't feel anxiety at times over things, especially when I want to see someone avoid a mistake I've made. But I also remind myself that all the so called mistakes I've made have led me to where I am today. I doubt I'd have learned my lessons any other way. But of course I had also bought into many mistaken beliefs, most notably unworthiness and separation from God. Much, if not most, of my struggle and pain has been derived from what I'd chosen, and what had been chosen for me, to believe. What might my life look like had I understood these things years earlier? Different, very different. But truthfully, I do love my life today. If the only way to get here was going through all that stuff (and obviously it was) then I'd gladly do it all over again. It's been worth every tear, fear, rejection, doubt, and pain I've ever experienced, and I still consider it a bargain! What a deal—I've been given so much more than any price I've "paid"!

So, in a nutshell, this is why we come into this life with all we need, and then forget it's there. The journey, and the value we come to place on it, is in the rediscovery! And that doesn't happen overnight. While it is freely given to us by God, and always available to us, it's only in the long, slow, arduous climb out of our own darkness that we come to recognize the value of it.

I'll end this chapter by paraphrasing the ball player and little kid.

me: "Hey God, why is it so hard to get good at life?"

God: "Well, being hard is what makes it so great!"

Exactly!

6

Purpose

o o o o o o o o o o o o o o o o o o o o o o o o o o o o o o o o o o
*"Your vision will become clear only when you look into your heart.
Who looks outside, dreams. Who looks inside, awakens."*

—*Carl Jung*

Each one of us has something that we do better than anyone else in the
world. Really—I'm not kidding. This is absolutely true! Each one of us
has a unique way of doing something that is peculiar only to us. And
it's one of the reasons we're here on the earth at this moment. But *most
of us don't believe it!* The first problem we run up against we touched on
in the last chapter. This ability (or talent) was "freely" given to us and,
because it is second nature, we usually don't see it as anything special.
We ignore it or dismiss it. Of course there are those whose gifts are
obvious: the musical prodigy, the fabulous athlete, the person who is so
clearly gifted in art, or dance, or mathmatics, that it's virtually impossible to miss—they know it and so does everyone else. These people feel
that they *must* do this thing. It's not a matter of choice. In those cases
there's little doubt over what it is they will be doing with their lives. But
this is the exception, and it applies to very few of us.

Yet in truth, each one of us is a prodigy and virtuoso in something,
even if we don't see it. And we usually don't. The way never seems very
clear to us. If we're lucky, we wonder what it is we are meant to do. I

say "lucky" because it's really surprising how many of us *don't even ask* this vital question. Asking what it is we're meant for shows that we're at least wondering about "purpose". But most of us don't. Instead we look for the career track with the best pay plan and the most security. We seek the safe way. I do not dismiss the value of these things, because obviously they're important too. But if they're the only things we seek, there's a good chance we've set ourselves up for an unfulfilling life. Maybe even a miserable one. We should be asking ourselves questions like the following: What do I really enjoy? What am I good at? What really interests me? What can I see myself doing for years and never feeling bored? What makes me excited? What makes me wonder? What do I really want to know about? And perhaps one of the most telling questions of all: if I didn't get paid, would I still do this thing?

The answers to these questions points in a direction, but only if we listen. Unfortunately, many of us rarely do. Instead we listen to others' opinions of what we should do "for a living:" our parents, teachers, spouses, friends, and other usually well-intentioned people. The reason for this goes all the way back to what we learned long ago: we *don't* know and *"they"* do. And there's one other very powerful motivator as well: we want approval—often at any cost. Unfortunately, sometimes the price you pay is a life of trying to mold yourself to fit what you were never designed to fit *into*. You stay stuck at a place you were merely meant to pass through in order to *discover* what you didn't want to do for, and with, your life. But no matter how late it may seem to you, it is never too late to return to the gift *that you are* and what you were given to share with others. So, the task at hand is to look at the gifts you've been given: your natural abilities and talents. What have you overlooked and taken for granted?

Now, I'm not suggesting you pull the plug on your present life. I'm not advising you to quit your current job. You don't have to abandon your present life in order to fulfill your purpose. Where you currently find yourself is a part of that purpose. That may not be too comforting for you if you're struggling, but bear with me for a few minutes here. You have the life you have had for a reason. It has been your training ground, your classroom, and despite all appearances to the contrary—it's been given to you to prepare you, so it's given with nothing but love. That being said, you must ask yourself this: do I want to keep repeating the class over and over again? You are being called to wake up. You need to look deeply at what really matters to you. My guess is that if you are reading this, then you are probably interested in doing just that. You're asking yourself what it is you should be doing with this precious thing called your life.

Let me share some of what has happened with my life since those terrible days in 1991 and after that day on the hillside. You see, after being told the things I was told, it became apparent to me that all the things preceding that day had led me there. With that came a much deeper level of acceptance for things in my past, both good *and* bad. As I told you, on that day I did learn about my purpose. By delivering the message to you, I'm doing it. But I was also told there were other things I am to do, and that I already had all the essentials needed to accomplish them. After all, I'd been in training my whole life. At least that's what I was told. I was told that it was no accident that I'd found myself in the family I'd been born in to. I asked the question that seemed most obvious to me: what qualified me to do as I was being asked—and how would I be able to support my family? Again, no sooner had I dotted that question mark when the answer spilled out on to the paper:

You have always been given what you needed—always! Throughout your life—always! Why should this change? I have given you so much! Look at your gifts, the talents and abilities you have! They've

***been given to you for a reason. Use them! Stop looking elsewhere for
the answers. Use what has been given to you.***

For a good part of my adult life I'd believed the opposite of what this
told me. But by the time I'd made it to that hillside there was certainly
ample proof that I'd been provided for time and time again. All I
needed to do was look at my life. Yet as you already know, even with all
that proof, I still went to that hillside doubting myself and my direction. Of course, looking back with today's perspective, I can see what a
gift those feelings were. How else would I have gotten to that hillside?

One day while discussing the idea of life callings, a close friend of
mine commented that it was probably no coincidence that the job I had
held for so many years contained the word "service". Of course, when
I'd stumbled into that career I had no idea that the concept of service to
others would be important to me one day. But I did enjoy being helpful, and people seemed to find it easy to talk with me. I guess I was
what you'd call "accessible." I've always found it easy to strike up a conversation with just about anybody. I'd been raised by people who liked
to talk. Truth is, I had a very hard time *not* talking. Nobody in my family ever seemed to be at a loss for words, and frankly when I was little, I
had to work extra hard just to keep up with the pack. So the innate
ability I had to chat and put people at ease was something I'd never
seen as a gift or talent, but rather as just the way I was—nothing special.
After all, in my family we all were that way to a greater or lesser extent.
I took it for granted. It simply was the way *I was*. But I have come to
realize that not everybody is comfortable talking with people, and the
fact that it comes so easily to me *is* a gift.

By the mid 1990's I'd spent almost 10 years in a business I didn't
much care for any longer. Not that I didn't like being a service manager, and I did enjoy the people I worked with. But more and more it

seemed that my personal values and priorities were at odds with the industry I was in. The job had become merely what I did during the day in order to pay the bills. I had no passion for it and that didn't feel right to me. Doing something simply for the money, while at times necessary, takes its toll on you after awhile.

As the year 1995 got underway I started to ask myself in earnest what I should do about this. I knew it was time to make a break. But where? Then, seemingly out of the blue, a friend offered me a position with his company. His business had absolutely nothing to do with automobiles, and that was appealing. I decided to give it a try. But within a few months I found it was not a good fit for either one of us. It wasn't a matter of values this time, because we both shared those. It was really more about management styles. I valued our relationship more than a paycheck, and so did he, so we parted amicably. Of course there was one small problem: no job. There was nothing on the horizon that I could see. But I did know one thing, and I was sure of it: I had absolutely no desire to return to the automobile business. I asked myself "now what?". Then, only days after I'd left that job, I was asked by my Dad to help out managing his business affairs, which had become pretty tangled (and that's an understatement! Especially because it had always been my mother who kept the books). By 1995 my mom had already been in an Alzheimers care unit for almost three years, so things were a mess. Dad had never been a bookkeeper. While having been a successful businessman, he'd relied on others to handle the details. Here he was in his 80's, living all alone in the home we'd all grown up in, 2oo miles away from me. The house was a huge old place that, much like my parents, was showing the signs of age. It needed more care and attention than he was able to give it. It was time for a change and the house had to go. So that year, with the blessings of my sister and brother, I became the estate manager for our parents. It fell to me to finalize the sale of the family home, move my dad into a retirement community, disburse business assets and set up a financial team and attorney to assist me with all this. For the first year or so it was a full time job. I had a lot to learn. But I'd never made any pretense that I knew what I was doing. Fortunately I was able to hire a team of professionals to help me. I oversaw transactions, arranged services, signed checks and generally managed what my parents no longer could. With the passage of time the job settled down to part-time. This allowed me to pursue other options for my life.

Two significant events took place within a year of being asked to take care of my folks affairs. First I resumed playing music when an old friend and former bandmate moved down the street from me. Jane took up the bass guitar, and began sitting in when we got together to play some of the old songs. I was impressed with her ability to pick it up so quickly. But I probably shouldn't have been—after all, music was a passion of hers and she was definitely a natural. Within a few months we added a drummer. Amazingly, the band that grew out of these casual get-togethers has lasted over 8 years as of this writing and attracted a loyal following. This return to music has led me to things I'd never imagined possible once upon a time: the building of my own recording studio, and a small independent record label. I'm the only "signed" artist at the moment, but that's perfectly okay with me. I've taken what I've learned experimenting on my own recordings and began producing for others. This has allowed me to work with some talented local artists.

My return to music has also opened doors for doing other work as well. Again these are things I never would have seen for myself had not all these other things happened. In 1999 a good friend of mine volunteered me for work with a local teen mentoring program. A few months earlier I'd told him of a plan Jane had come up with that would offer schools a music mentoring program to help kids who were doing poorly or having problems. She envisioned it as a way to keep kids connected to school and as a way to motivate them. We'd gone so far as to write a proposal and present it to the high school in our town. While initially they seemed interested, after reviewing the proposal they decided to pass on it. I was working on another project at the time, so things never went any further. But I had told my buddy about our idea. When he got involved with the youth association in his town the following year, he brought up the idea to one of the counselors there. One thing led to another and before I knew it I was traveling to their high school a few days a week, seeing two guys who'd had their share of problems. While neither was very interested in school, they were interested in playing guitar, and that's where we made our connection. I'm happy to say that both have since graduated, a scenario that had seemed very much in doubt when I'd first met them. I'm hoping to be able to bring this program to other schools and communities in the future and am looking into getting funding.

Sadly, the second event was not so joyful. A very special man, my dear friend Pete, succumbed to cancer at the age of 42. For me he was the teacher who appeared when I, the student, was finally ready. I think most people can point to at least one person who had a profound effect on them, someone who changed their life and its direction. This is who Pete is to me—the turning point in my life. From our very first meeting until he became ill a few years later, he shared with me the things his life had taught him. And then he went even further: he guided me to my next "job." Through Pete's illness I saw, up close and personal, the work of Hospice and I immediately knew I wanted to do that kind of work. A year after Pete's death I had completed my training and was out in the field as a Hospice volunteer.

People always seem interested, and a bit surprised, when I tell them I work with Hospice. A question I hear often is: "Isn't that depressing? Doesn't it get to you—all that death?" My answer is always the same: on the contrary, it helps me. It reminds me that someday it'll be my turn, and that makes me want to live this moment as awake as I can be, to see and feel as much as I can. By recognizing the temporary nature of life, I purposefully live this day. I know tomorrow is not guaranteed! I believe that we can never truly live until we accept that one day we will die—at least to this life. This work with Hospice has been much more than work to me. It's been *purpose*. I feel all the things I've been given freely—all my natural abilities—get put to use as I do this, and I feel blessed by the people I have met through my work.

So, I'm not sure whether I found a way, or it was the other way around and the way found me. But whichever it was, I've been able to take my experiences and share them in the service of others, and that has been a gift—mostly to me, I might add. My experiences in and with music became something I was able to "give" to another person. And the lessons I'd learned through some of my own rash decisions regarding the importance of school were shared with the young men I began seeing weekly as we played guitar together. Has it changed their lives? I don't know. But I know it's changed mine. And that change continues for me.

Today playing music is a very different experience for me. What motivates me today is in stark contrast to years earlier, when visions of celebrity, wealth and adulation were the driving factors. Quite frankly, today I'm thrilled just being able to play again! *And* that so many people seem to enjoy what we do! A story from one of the people who routinely comes to see our band brought this all home to me. I'd like to share it with you here; if only to illustrate this: we never know how something we may take for granted or consider commonplace might actually help another person.

One night Kate brought her sister, Carolyn, (both names have been changed) who had never seen us, out to dance. Carolyn had been in a terrible marriage to a very abusive man for many years, and she'd finally worked up enough courage to leave him and start her life over. That night they had a blast, and Carolyn danced to practically every song we played. She had such a good time that she promised to come out again. But sadly she never made it back. Tragically, just a few weeks later she was murdered by her husband. I'm shocked and saddened by her death, but touched by the fact that in a life that was such a struggle, a few hours of music gave her some joy and pleasure. Kate later told us that she hadn't seen her sister do that much dancing since they'd been teenagers. She'd also not seen her sister smile and laugh so much in years. To me this story, although quite sad, really brought home to me that playing music for people is a privilege. To bring some joy to peoples lives by giving them a fun night out is an honor.

But before you pronounce me Saint Richard, I should tell you that I still struggle with some of my old behaviors and reactions. I can still be self-centered more often than I'd like to admit to you. There are even times I balk at the idea of volunteering for anything, feeling that my time is already spread too thin. But then I take a few deep breaths and remind myself of what I know to be true today: we are here to help one another. Pete had taught me that by even taking only a few minutes, we can help someone else. So in those times when I feel overwhelmed and don't want to do anything, I go back to starting small, and I simply do one thing. I remind myself that it's okay not to do *everything*, that it doesn't have to be *all* of it. Just one thing is fine—just one little thing is a very good beginning, and that's what it's all about: beginning. A good portion of my life I had felt lousy about myself because I did nothing.

The reason I did nothing was easy to explain: why bother? It was too big, and what could little old me do anyway? I never saw any middle ground. It was either all or nothing! And because I couldn't do the big things that might really change the world, I did nothing instead. What a waste! One of the most important things I've ever learned is this: helping another human being can be the tiniest thing. Sometimes just a smile; sometimes simply letting another person know that you appreciated them may change the world.

So ask yourself what your talents are. What is it that you seem to be good at? Don't dismiss it as unimportant. And don't say you're not good at anything. And most importantly—don't judge it. Let go of what others have told you that you "should" do. Ask yourself what you *can* do—for yourself *and* for another. Ask what you can give. Ask to be shown, and promise to be willing to be open to what you are shown. Then go about your life as if everything you do matters, *because it does*! While you are doing your best to live honorably and ethically, keep asking what you can give rather than what you can get. You will be led to what you're called to do. And when the way finds you, you will find a way to do it! Trust this.

I'd like to end this chapter with a quote that really speaks to the idea that often the things we may take for granted, and not see as special, may help another human being when we step forward and share it:

If I am blind, I can run my hand across the back of a shell and celebrate beauty. If I have no legs, I can sit in quiet wonder before the restless murmurs of the sea. If I am wounded in spirit, I can reach out my hand to those who are hurting. If I am lonely, I can go among those who are desperate for love. There is no tragedy or injustice so great, no life so small and inconsequential, that we cannot bear witness to the light in the quiet acts and hidden moments of our days.

And who can say which of these acts and moments will make a difference? The universe is vast and is a magical membrane of meaning, stretching across time and space, and it is not given to us to know her secrets and her ways. Perhaps we were placed here to meet the challenge of a single moment; perhaps the touch we give will cause the touch that will change the world-
Anonymous

Your gift is the experience of your life. Share that, and you share the greatest gift any of us can give to another. And that <u>is</u> purpose!

7

DYING

On September 11th, 2001 my daughter Michelle, who lives on Long Island, called me to see how I was doing. I was okay, but it was clear to me that she was pretty rattled. She asked me if the events of that day might mean that the end of the world was coming. She'd heard people talking about the start of World War Three. She was scared, just like a lot of other people. These events always seem to bring out those people I call "doomsdayers"—the ones who say that God is punishing us because we've strayed, or that whatever it is that's happening was foretold thousands of years ago, fulfilling prophesy, so you better get ready because the end is near. I told her I didn't believe any of those things. We talked back and forth about the events of that terrible day and what they might mean to our country and the world. As we continued talking the tone of her voice changed, as her words slowed, becoming more thoughtful.

"Dad, I realized as I watched the towers burning and saw people jumping, that those people had no idea when they started their day a few hours earlier that it would be their last day. I thought about the planes and the people who thought they were on their way to wherever they were going, fully expecting to get there. I realized that I take it for granted when I get into my car, or go to work, or start my day, that I'll arrive back home at night and get to do it all over again." She let the last words trail off. I sat there waiting for her to continue. I could almost "feel" her thinking, choosing her next words.

"You know Dad, today I "got" that I'm going to die someday. I mean, I know that sounds funny, because of course I'm going to die—we all know that it's inevitable. But what I mean is that today *I really got it*—deep down inside of me-I *knew it*! I realized that this whole thing—this whole life—is just really, *really*, temporary."

At the age of 20 she had a moment of clarity, an understanding of an unavoidable reality of life. The fog of denial had melted away and Michelle looked at her own mortality.

I imagine that there were similar discussions going on all across America. Death had been brought home to all of us. We knew we could be next, and it might happen in a heartbeat. We could be at work, on the train, in our car, or at the mall. Anyplace might be our last place. But did that awareness last? Part of being human is that we forget—we go on to the "next" thing. This forgetting is our defense. Death scares us. Maybe all the noise, all the "stuff" in our modern world, is really just our meager attempt to keep the bogeyman away—like a kid whistling as he walks past the cemetery at night.

If we allow ourselves to experience some stillness, turn off the radio and the TV and sit with the quiet, what happens? We get restless—we begin to squirm a bit. A minute stretches out, and where we once felt as if there was not enough time, now it feels as if there's too much! That minute feels as if its 10 minutes. Time slows, drags, seems to crawl at a snails pace. So why the discomfort? Why is it so damn hard to sit still? Training. Do you remember being punished as a kid by being made to sit still? Early on most of us learned to associate this idea with some form of punishment! Talk about having things backwards! The truth is: in silence we are left with our own precious self. But because of all our past conditioning, based on that one faulty premise of unworthiness, we have never seen that *it is* precious. God forbid we get to really know ourselves! And if we allowed that, then we might actually allow ourselves to know others, and in turn allow them to know us. And *that* might lead to deeply caring, which in turn leads to pain, because when we see another suffer, it is no longer mere sympathetic words as we say "I feel your pain," it is a heart that aches *with* that pain. Because in that shared experience and knowing, there is vulnerability, and of course, loss, the ultimate loss being death itself. Yet, like so many other things we have been afraid of throughout our lives, this too is really nothing more than an imaginary monster under the bed. Death holds no real power over any of us unless we allow it to, and we only do this when we deny it.

Let me ask you: would you live today—this very day—differently if you reminded yourself that there will come a time when you will no longer be here in this world? What does that realization do to the relationships and events in your life right now? How does your life look? What about your priorities? What words would you say if you knew that tomorrow you'd no longer be able to speak them? Who would you call? What does this do to the things you see every day? Do you see them differently when you really get that this time might be the last time you get to look at them with the eyes you now have? I'll bet it does. It has to. That awareness brings you to see things as you've never seen them before. To *really* see them.

But once again let me remind you: you who are reading this will never die. The eyes that see this page will waste away and decompose, but you who are now using them will not. So, the simple truth is this: death is nothing to fear. Especially when you come to know that you are worthy and always have been. See how we always return to this? Death only frightens us if we fear punishment of some kind for having done "wrong" things and for disappointing God, or because we fear annihilation and nonexistence. Neither of those things is any more than fearful imaginings. At the root of much suffering is this fear of death, and we do whatever we can to avoid it. Perversely, this fear, which leads to all sorts of denial, actually prevents us from living our lives fully.

Do you really want to change your life right now—today—this very instant? Pretend you're dead. I'm not kidding. Imagine the world without you. Take a few moments in silence, just sitting, and seeing things without the "you" you are today. Now acknowledge and accept as fully as is possible that this will be true someday, and that you have no idea when that day may be. Tomorrow is guaranteed to no one. As you go though your day, remind yourself of this often. This is not about being morose or depressive; it's about living now—today—this moment. It changes what matters to you. Maybe not right away, but it will as you practice this reminding. So many things you once believed to be important or necessary, seem to fizzle and fade as you do this. I love the following quote, which to me sums up what is learned when we make friends with death. There is a saying: *A man who plants a tree sapling knowing full well that he will never sit and enjoy its shade truly understands life's meaning.* We are each here to make the world a better place. That's our assignment. *Remembering* this puts much of life's apparent troubles into perspective.

Here's another suggestion. The next time you're in your car, turn off the radio. Drive in silence and notice things. You see, choosing silence is possible. Here's someplace where you get to choose. For most of us, as soon as we turn the key in the ignition, the sound of music, news commentator, or DJ jumps out at us, because we probably never even turn the stereo off. It's all automatic! But it doesn't have to be. I've actually found that driving in silence can be almost like meditation. It's amazing what happens when you turn stuff off! Try it at home as well. To paraphrase the psychedelic guru of the 1960's, Dr. Timothy Leary: **Turn off** all the devices and all the noise that distracts you. **Tune in** to that still small voice within you, the one that can only be heard when we get very, very quiet.

Drop out of the routines you've developed in your life that keep you on the go and constantly "doing."

You may discover that you get some remarkable thoughts percolating when you allow yourself to practice this. But this can't happen unless you give it space to happen *in*. It's about being conscious and making that choice. It's always up to you, but you must be willing to notice what you are doing in order to be able to choose. One of the great gifts that stillness and silence can bring us is awareness. There is no way that the still small voice that resides within each of us can compete with the clatter of the modern world. That's why you must give that voice the space it needs in order to come forth for you. That voice is connected to God, and it is within you.

The ego has trouble sitting still and being quiet. And as you know, it wants you to believe that it is you. That's why it tries to keep you distracted with all kinds of thoughts and things to do. Why do you think there's so much of everything in our culture? Because it's a culture totally *driven* by the ego. The ego believes that by always staying busy it gets to stay in control and avoid death. But the ego is tied to your body. With the body's death, the ego will also cease to be of use. If the thought of the loss of your body upsets you, try to think of it as if it were a car. You use your car to get you from place to place. Of course the connection to your body is much stronger than your connection to your car—at least I hope it is! But you see my point. Just as when the time comes and your car no longer serves you, you pull it over and park it, shut off the engine and get out one last time. So to will you one day park your body and get out—like slipping off an old coat. But what might that be like if you're minus the ego? Will you even know? Well, I'll bet you've already experienced life beyond the ego. In moments we all do. If you've ever forgotten yourself, been so completely absorbed in something that you lost all sense of time, and everything else for that matter, then you've been beyond the ego. Many people describe this state as complete peace or bliss. We commonly say something like "I forgot myself", or "I lost track of time", in order to describe it. Beyond the ego you are completely present and in *that* moment, and that is all there is! That's why nothing else interferes—there <u>is</u> nothing else! The present moment is eternal because in truth nothing else is real—the present moment is all there is. Don't think so? Well, where does the past exist? In your memory. And the future? In your imagination. Stepping outside the ego, there is nothing to take us away from the present and in that present is also the Presence. Death returns us to our Source and that is the Present. We go back to that from which we came: God.

To me the perfect metaphor for God is the ocean: huge, mighty, powerful. We are within that ocean. Take a glass and scoop some water at the shore. What is in that glass? It is the same thing. Yet it would be foolish to think that the water in that glass could swamp a ship. But pour that glass back into the waves and now what is possible? The same is true of you.

What might dying be like? My guess is that in the final moments it will seem very familiar, and we will be surprised at the ease of it. One moment we'll be here, and the next moment, "there." Hundreds of people who have been clinically dead (no heartbeat, no brain activity) and then resuscitated have told of very similar experiences: the continuation of consciousness and awareness, along with a sense of absolute peace and complete love. There are numerous books recounting these cases in detail. Doctors Raymond Moody and Melvin Morse are two of the many professionals who have conducted in-depth research into the near death experience. Their books are part of an ever growing body of work dealing with this subject.

But what about us as individuals? When we return to God does that mean that the "we" that we were, is gone? Yes, in the sense of the limited-perspective, three dimensional being you once were; no, in the sense of all that you truly are and have ever been. Will you know this? While I cannot speak from personal experience (at least none that I can recall), by all indications and considering what I was told on that hillside, I would have to answer with an unequivocal "Yes." You will not only know, but you will fully experience the truth: you are as you've always been and always will be. And what about "there?" Same answer: "there" has always been "here" as well, only now you will see and know this as well. What of others—departed loved ones? All are aspects of what you are, and yes, they will be there as well. And what can you expect to experience? Your own totality. And of course whatever else you choose. You do not end.

In this and the preceding chapters I have shared with you the message I received along with some of my personal experiences, in the hope that they may help you on your own journey. In the next chapter I will share the daily practices that have made a profound difference in the quality of my life.

8

Practices Guaranteed To Improve Your Life

1. Forgiveness
2. Acceptance
3. Gratitude
4. Don't Judge
5. Live Now
6. Be Congruent
7. Choose the Thoughts You Keep
8. Expand Your God Consciousness
Through Prayer and Meditation

At the top of the list is my favorite "F" word:

1 Forgiveness. All the things you try to "do" to become more spiritually fit, whether it be meditating 2 hours a day, praying, fasting, spiritual books, vision quests, seminars, gurus, retreats, will all fall flat until you are able to do this one thing: forgive. First yourself, and then everyone and everything else. If someone does not forgive you it should not change your forgiving yourself and them as well. What they do is not your concern. What *you do,* is.

Forgiveness does not mean excusing. But healing cannot take place without it. If someone has caused you harm, abused you, stolen from you, whatever they may have done, forgiving them does not mean they are free from consequences for the acts they've committed. But you cease being the judge, jury, and executioner. You may believe that there are things that can never be forgiven-terrible acts, horrendous things. The terrible acts and the horrendous things need not be forgiven-only the person who may have performed them. Each and every human being started out the same way: an innocent infant, wanting only to be loved and to be accepted. Then, whatever happened to them happened, and they lost their way. Despise the sin, but don't hate the sinner. When Jesus was asked by one of the disciples if they were to forgive someone as many as seven times, Jesus replied that they should forgive 70 times 70, and more. Forgive as much as needed. Amen to that.

2 Acceptance. Acceptance is not approving of anything and everything. It is merely acknowledging *what is*. Acceptance helps you define the things you can, and cannot, change. Change happens when we see what "is" and then acknowledge the need to change it. And here is a vitally important point: if we see what "is" and, in that seeing, realize that we are powerless to change it, then that frees us up from having to *be in resistance* to it. The practice of *not* accepting always puts us in conflict against whatever it is we're resisting. It gives that thing we're resisting power. What we resist, persists.

Have you ever gotten stuck in heavy traffic, bumper to bumper and stop and go? How do you feel? At peace? I doubt it. Most of us respond in a similar way. Physiologically, blood pressure climbs, stomach tenses, jaw clenches. You may grip the wheel tighter and look for what's causing the traffic mess. If you're supposed to be someplace at a set time, you're probably looking at the clock on the dashboard or your watch every few minutes. Is there anything you can do to change the way the traffic is? No. But I'll bet you don't even think of this. Instead you probably curse the situation, get more angry as the seconds slip by, and focus all your attention on this thing you have no control over: the traffic. The traffic cares not that it's inconvenienced you. The traffic simply is what it is: traffic, doing what traffic sometimes does, clog up and crawl along.

But what happens if you let go and accept what is at that moment? Things improve! Your clenched jaw relaxes. You take a slow and deliberate deep breath and your stomach muscles ease a bit. What can you control? Your attitude. *And therein lies power!* Given any situation, you can choose to *not be* in resistance to what is. This sounds so simple. It is. But simple *does not* mean easy! And because it is simple does not diminish its value. But learning to change your typical response to one of acceptance is priceless.

When we resist and struggle, we accomplish very little aside from making ourselves crazier and crazier. Returning to our traffic scenario: by letting go of your resistance you "un-plug" yourself from the growing anger and tension that's being carried by so many of your fellow motorists, who are probably doing anything and everything but practicing this thing called acceptance. By your act of disconnecting from the emotional torment, you do your part to change the situation. This is true even for the people who haven't a clue that you've taken a deep breath and accepted what is. Remember: our thoughts have real power, and we do not exist in a vacuum. Consider the following example.

Have you ever had the experience of walking into a room full of people and felt tension so thick it could be cut by a knife? You had no idea what had gone on there, but you felt the atmosphere, and clearly something was not right. Maybe two people had just had a heated exchange. Whatever the cause, you could feel the "charge" in the air around you. That's what I'm talking about here! It's the same principle. We each transmit what's happening inside of us. We may think we hide it, but it leaks out into the world around us. *What we think and what we hold inside ourselves affects those around us.* Now multiply this by 6 billion!

What happens to the atmosphere around us if 500 million of us are angry and tense? How about if 300 million of us are afraid?

You see: not only do you owe it to yourself, but you owe it to the whole of humanity to learn to practice acceptance! Am I saying you should never be upset? Absolutely not. There are even times when we need to become upset. Often change doesn't happen until we do become upset enough to take action. But we should always ask ourselves what we can change and what we cannot. Traffic, the weather, interest rates, the stock market, or time—especially the past—are all good examples of things we allow to upset and control us, yet we have no control over. And that is a waste of energy, effort, and the most precious thing of all: your life.

3 Gratitude. This practice has become one of my favorites. When I feel out of touch with how good my life is, this practice plugs me back in, and with that things always begin to improve for me. No matter how dark my mood might be, my attitude gets better and then things around me seem to miraculously transform themselves. But given the power of our thoughts, this is really no surprise. After all, we are involved in what shows up in our life. By tapping into the energy that gratitude brings us, we set our lives on a better course. By saying "thank you," we are acknowledging to the universe, and to our Source, that we have good in our life. We are saying "it is so," and that is what will be.

But how can you really be grateful when it seems like everything in your life is going wrong? How can you be grateful when there seems nothing to be grateful for? You start small. You begin with the basics: air to breathe, sunshine to warm you, or rain and clouds to cool you off. How about your senses? Touch, smell, sight: if they all work, then you've got much to be thankful for. If only some work, you still have something to be grateful for. What about the rest of your health? Is it relatively good? If so, say thanks. If not, say thanks anyway. I know this may sound crazy, but it works. When my life was really unraveling and everything looked bleak to me, my friend Pete introduced me to this practice. He suggested I write a list of everything I was grateful for. I told him it'd be a really short list! I felt I had very little to be thankful for. He said I should do it anyway. He even gave me a few things to get started with-some of the same ones I've given you. Anyway, I made a start. With time the list has only grown. Today I have moments when I feel so grateful for all I've been given that it feels as though my heart could actually burst.

This practice changes the way you see things. Once again, it's all about perspective. As you start to become aware of the things to be thankful for, even more things to be grateful for begin to show up in your life. It's as if your life becomes "magnetized" to attract good things! Of course this is why your thoughts are so important. They are the "magnet." Staying positive and looking to see the good in situations keeps you "attractive". But I don't want to mislead you here. I'm not saying bad stuff (or at least what you believe to be "bad") won't show up in your life, because it will. However, as you continually practice this new attitude concerning gratitude, you'll build up your gratitude "muscle". Even in the midst of troubles, you'll instinctively know that things will ultimately be all right. Your experiences will teach you that often troubles lead to blessings. By practicing this you will be reminding yourself. And you tap into the things you have right at that moment to be grateful for. This will hold you and help you through whatever the difficulty happens to be. And that changes everything.

This practice will help you through the most difficult of times. It's not about denying the difficulty of the circumstances. It's about accepting them, and looking beyond them. It's about *not getting stuck in the problem or difficulty*, but being available for the solution and gift. And it's about seeing what's right with your life even when so many things might seem wrong.

4 Don't Judge. Mid-20th century Belgian poet Maurice Maeterlinck said the following about judging people: "I have never once seen clearly within myself. How then would you have me judge the deeds of others?". Getting sucked into judging others is a way for us to avoid ourselves. That's what's so attractive about it, and why we so often fall into that behavior. Remember this: judging is a function of the ego, and the ego is insecure. It will find fault outside itself (you) wherever possible. So, if I'm looking at you and you're more successful (i.e. more money, better job, bigger house, newer car, etc.), my ego wants to level the playing field. It will try to do that. Maybe that's why there's this new trend in TV shows. They give us a chance to see rich and successful people who are not very appealing; the so called "unscripted" real life adventures of whoever is selected this week. We get to look at them and feel smug. After all, we're certainly not as stupid, selfish, shallow, greedy, or whatever the show is pitching to land its audience. But this is a trap that far too many of us have fallen in to. When we're engaged in judgment, we're wasting our time. Trying to feel better about ourselves by feeling superior or hateful toward someone else doesn't work. Unfortunately, today millions of us are being drugged by this kind of "entertainment."

None of us has any more than 24 hours in a day. So with this in mind, how much time could you make available for yourself by eliminating this activity of judging? As you've already learned: you are as important as they come! As worthy as they come! It's already a done deal, and there's no need to run another person down and then compare yourself in order to feel better about yourself.

But there are other kinds of judging as well, and of course daily life requires that we evaluate things; we do need to assess risks and actions.

These things are necessary and not what I'm referring to when I say don't judge. What about world events? political situations, economic ups and downs, tragedies and catastrophe's? It's not that you won't have thoughts and opinions on these because of course you will. But remember: when we make something either "good" or "bad" we limit our understanding. And we often become a prisoner of the emotions we may attach to this. The truth to all situations is that we all only see a narrow picture of what is. Of the grand scheme of the universe, and the cause and effect on future events, we know practically nothing at all.

5 Live in the Present. It's the only place you can be isn't it? No. Surprisingly, most of us don't spend a lot of time here. We're usually somewhere back in our past replaying some scene or event, or we're up ahead of ourselves, worrying about or wishing for something. The present moment is a place we rarely are. If you don't think so, then I suggest you start paying attention. Ask yourself where you are throughout your day. As you begin to pay attention, I think you will be surprised by what you find. How much of life have you been missing because you've been somewhere else? The present moment is the only one that is real! The past and future exist only in your mind. With this awareness you begin to see every moment as unique. This is a sacred perspective. You become conscious that this moment, this "now," will never be again. Present moment awareness is definitely not a natural inclination of ours. God knows we've created enough things to tear ourselves away from it. So your challenge each day, in each moment, is to remind yourself of this, to bring yourself back to this.

This is a daunting challenge. But don't let it intimidate you! This is not about doing this perfectly. None of these practices is. I don't know if it is even possible to do it perfectly! So far I certainly haven't. Not even close. I can only guess how often I am truly present in the moment on a day-to-day basis. But here's the thing: when it does happen, I know it, and it is powerful! And man, is it worth all the effort! What does it feel like to be truly present? Well, If you're over the age of 50 I'll bet you remember exactly where you were when you heard that JFK had been shot. Thinking about it right now I'll bet you can call up your emotional reaction of the time, and maybe even re-experience it. That's present moment awareness. In that moment, you were *there*. Today a whole new generation will be able to do the same when the subject of September 11th comes up.

These two examples use tragic events. Unfortunately, they are the things that so often bring us "present." There is no denying that life can be painful, but it can also be amazingly joyful. If we did not have the pain, would we even recognize the joy? By bringing your awareness back to the present moment, your life will become richer than you've ever imagined. Just by asking yourself throughout your day, "where am I right at this moment?" you will began to be more conscious in your life.

This practice is not meant to be a way to avoid the future by failing to plan or take responsibility. In truth, when we are present in the moment we *are* taking responsibility. We should always strive to be as conscious as possible when attempting to plan or map out our future. By doing this, the future will become a place in which we all get to flourish!

6. Be Congruent. What this means is: what I say, what I do, and who I am are all in agreement with one another. Most of us don't realize the effect inconsistencies have in our lives-the toll they take on our self image as the subconscious mind keeps track of everything. When we say one thing but do something else, we pay a price. On a deep level we learn that our word is not important, not trustworthy. That affects how our life feels to us. And this will sabotage us when we set a goal or attempt to change things for the better in our life. Because the subconscious mind has observed that we don't mean what we say, it concludes that when we promise ourselves that we're going to do something we really don't mean it. Guess what happens? We don't accomplish what we'd hoped to, and the cycle gets reinforced and starts all over again. Developing congruence changes this.

I know I keep coming back to this, but it's probably one of the most important things you can ever know: what we believe about ourselves affects every aspect of our life. You know the price we've paid by believing in our unworthiness. The same thing applies here, and it can trip your life up without you having a clue as to why things always seem to go poorly for you. When you do what you say, and this is in agreement with how you feel and what you believe, you are in harmony. As a musician, I like harmony. Most people do. You don't need to know a thing about music to recognize it. Why? Because it's *pleasing* to the ear. The combination of notes work together. They don't fight one another. Again, having absolutely no knowledge of music, you know when notes don't work, when the pitch is off, because you can hear it. It sounds bad and it clashes. That's called dissonance. Strive for congruency, because that will lead to harmony.

7 Choose the thoughts you wish to keep. Thoughts come of their own accord. You can't choose what shows up. Some people might disagree with me about this. They may believe they choose every thought they think. If they'd like to believe that, then so be it. As for me, I see it differently. Thoughts pop into my mind all the time, and I often have no idea why I just happened to think one at that particular moment.

Personally I believe this is what the mind does: it likes to stay busy. Buddhists have a saying: "monkey mind." It's probably because one day some monk observed the way monkeys run about and chatter a lot. Our minds are like that, always rummaging about, looking for stuff. Thoughts come and go, often very rapidly. But when one of them catches our attention we grab on with all our might. And this can be either good news or bad news, depending of course on what the thought is. This is where the choice comes in. Often most of us don't realize that we have a choice. Once that thought has gotten our attention, it's as if we've put a searchlight on it, and all our energies are directed there. This can be damaging if the thought happens to be a negative or fear based one with little basis in reality (yet).

But we don't have to do this. When a thought comes into our awareness we can ask a few questions to help us choose whether to stay with it or send it on its way. "Is it positive or fearful?" is a great place to start. If your experience is anything like mine, once you start paying attention you'll be amazed at how many are fear-based.

When I was told this I began noticing the thoughts that showed up. I was blown away. It was practically every other thought that happened by. Out of nowhere would come a question: had I entered the correct number at the bottom of page 2 on last year's taxes? and immediately I would go to "audit". It didn't have to be near April 15th for this to happen. There was no correlation. That's what I saw time and again. There didn't need to be any correlation to anything in reality. All there needed to be was my willingness to latch on to the thought. The thought would just pop in, and then I'd start to run with it. I'd be out on the lake, floating along in my kayak. The sun shining, the sky brilliantly blue, and all of a sudden, wham! "What will I do if the country goes into a depression?" and I was off to the races once more. So learning this was really a godsend for me. I've trained myself to notice when I begin to do this, and then I interrupt the whole process. I stop and get off, I don't follow any of these thoughts out to their "logical" conclusions. Instead I remind myself I can choose to let the thought go. That way I get to choose to stay on the water and enjoy the sun.

There are all sorts of negative thoughts that will bombard you all day long, every hour, every second or two. Don't make them welcome. Recognize them and send them packing. Turn your thoughts to something *you* choose—or even better—return yourself to the moment you are in. Become present.

Thoughts can come from other sources as well. What do you watch on TV? What type of movies? What about the radio? As my kids got older and beyond the reach of what I deemed acceptable, they began to watch some really terrible stuff. Some of it was violent, some of it just mindless trash, practically all of it negative in tone. One day I asked my daughter if she would eat poison everyday. Ask yourself that same question. Would you expect your body to be healthy if you fed it large amounts of junk food with a few dabs of poison on the side every day? Why should any of us expect anything different from our mind? The mind is like a sponge, it soaks up things. Become conscious that what you feed it has an effect on it. I monitor what I allow in.

Now this is not about putting your head in the sand and ignoring difficult and troubling subject matter. It's vital that we look at what is happening. But it's equally vital that we do not bathe ourselves in a constant sea of negativity, because it will drown us. Limit your intake. Being out in the sun is a good thing. Too much sun isn't. It's the same here. Choose what you focus on. Choose the thoughts you wish to stay with. Developing this awareness has made a big difference for me in my life, and I think you'll feel the same way.

8 Expand Your God Consciousness: Pray and Meditate Daily. I thought about putting this first on the list, but these practices are not in order of importance. They're *all* important! As for this one: ten years ago, if anyone had told me that I'd be getting up at 5:30 in the morning so I could spend my first hour of the day in prayer and meditation, I probably wouldn't have believed them. Yet today I would sooner skip my first cup of coffee and breakfast than do without this time. You don't have to do as I do and get up at such an early hour. But for me there is something very special, even sacred, about this time of day. That's why I love doing this. It is starting my day on the right foot.

There is no set method to this, no formula I can give you. I believe that prayer is a deeply personal thing, a living thing. I say "living" because it will evolve and develop as you do it. Personally, I don't use any of the formal prayers that I learned as a kid. Today I use only two prayers written by someone else. They are:

The Serenity Prayer:

God Grant me the serenity to accept the things I cannot change, the courage to change the things I can, and the wisdom to know the difference.

The Prayer of St. Francis:

Lord, make me a channel of thy peace: where there is hatred let me bring love, where there is wrong, I may bring the spirit of forgiveness; that were there is discord, I may bring harmony; that were there is error, I may bring truth; that were there is doubt, I may bring faith; that were there is despair, I may bring hope; that were there are shadows, I may bring light; that were there is sadness, I may bring joy. Lord grant that I may comfort rather than be comforted—to understand, rather than be understood—to love, than be loved. For it is by self forgetting, that one finds. It is by forgiving that one is forgiven. It is by dying that one awakens to Eternal Life. Amen

But you don't need to do what I do. It's about developing a relationship with *your* Higher Power, *your* Source, *the God of your understanding*. The only way to build any kind of relationship is by spending time together. You know God is always there, but how often do you acknowledge that? That's what I'm recommending. Talk to God, tell

God what's going on in your life, what you're feeling. Ask for guidance, and then trust that it'll show up. Ask God to show you.

Part of why I like the prayer of St. Francis so much is because of the things it asks: let me be an instrument of peace; let me love rather than be loved, forgive rather than be forgiven. But you'll find your own way. All you need do is make the time. God will do the rest.

As for meditation: the goal here is to simply sit in stillness for a period of time. For me, there is no other agenda here. I don't recommend that you try to "not think". Just sit and breathe. Notice your breath. Thoughts will come and go; just let them. Try not to latch on to any of them. There is no right way to do this, and the only wrong way is to not do it!

Meditation will change, just as your experience of prayer does, because it is also alive. All you need to do is show up, make time, and then do it. It may be helpful to select a reading that inspires you and think about that as you begin. I have a daily reflections book that has a different reading for every day of the year, and reading it is part of my practice before I begin to meditate.

So there you have them: 8 practices that will enrich your life. Notice the word practice, because that is the key. Change does not happen overnight. You don't plant a tomato seed and expect the plant there the next day. The same applies here. Practice is just that: you continually do these things in spite of how you might feel. How did you learn to ride a bike? How does a pianist go from the living room to symphony hall? And, even more importantly, once he's there, what must he continue to do if he wants to stay there? P-R-A-C-T-I-C-E. So, when you don't feel like doing these, just remind yourself of this. Trust me, you'll be glad you did.

9

Where To End?

Before I was able to write what you've read here, I had to crawl through a whole load of past—*my* past; to write the story of what happened to me ten years prior. This then grew into what I hadn't wanted to write at all, but did anyway—a semi-autobiography (a few bits of which did sneak their way into this book). That book evolved into a quasi self-help book that really wasn't "self" help at all, at least the small "s" self. I wrote a lot during the past three and a half years. Had I not used recycled paper I'd have been responsible for the death of far too many trees.

In my list of things I'd done for work in the beginning of this book, I failed to mention that I'd taken a stab at writing as well. When I was in my 30's I began writing short stories, mainly fiction. I also did some free-lance work for a local newspaper, writing human interest pieces and an Op-Ed or two. Both those things were much easier than writing this book. Fiction allowed my mind to play. Nothing was on the line for me; it was all make believe. As I wrote my stories, I often felt as if I were reading someone else's work, not sure what was coming next. I'd anxiously sit down to write because I wanted to see what would happen.

But my writing career was short lived. After having only my newspaper work published, I turned my attention to the matter at hand—trying to save a crumbling marriage and all the other troubles that converged on me in 1991. Not that I stopped writing, because I didn't. Only the stuff I wrote wasn't intended for publication—it was for me.

Hoping to sort out what was happening to my life, and trying to hang on to my own sanity, I started writing a journal. Writing helped me to sort through things, and it led me to look at my life and how I'd gotten to where I'd wound up. I kept a detailed record of all the things that started happening in my life as things came apart back in those early days of the 1990's.

As things unfolded during those terrible/wonderful months I realized something *strange* was going on. Events, people, and situations began appearing, as if by magic—right on cue and exactly when I needed them. This was when my friend Pete, about whom I spoke briefly in this book, showed up in my life. All the things that lined up in order to help me through that time were nothing short of miraculous. And after being "saved" (from myself as much as anything else), like so many people who have actually survived something they were certain was going to do them in, I wanted to tell others. More than that, I wanted to let others know that they could survive, too. Having been so obviously helped by the things I'd used to get through this awful time in my life, I had all the zeal of a revival tent preacher! I was on fire and wanted to spread the word—to share all the things I'd been shown. That's what I originally set out to do.

Initially I did this by talking with others. Then one day, as the ending of the century approached, I got the urge to have a look at some of my old writings. The turning of the millenium was prodding me. Changing centuries can do that, I guess. Anyway, I remembered my old journal and wanted to give it a read. It had been kept on floppy discs—the old kind that really were floppy. They were packed away in a box alongside my now ancient IBM clone computer, stored down in our basement. So I went down to the workshop and took the computer down off the shelf, wiped off all the dust, and hooked it up.

I was bit nervous because I thought I'd forgotten how to boot the thing up. Truthfully I had my doubts about the thing even running. A few pops, crackles and whirring sounds and the monitor came on. I half expected a puff of smoke. Anyway, I reached into the box and took out the discs containing my journal. There were over a dozen of them, along with some of my short stories. I looked at the labels and selected journal number one, flipped up the drive door and slid it in. A few more whirring clicks and there on the screen in front of me, flickering in yellow, glowing letters silhouetted against a dark background, were the words I'd written almost 10 years earlier. I began to read. The words were those of a confused, bewildered and frightened man who clearly thought the end of the world was at hand. Would he survive? Could he survive? And if so, then what?

As I read, I felt compassion for this poor guy I used to be, thinking to myself: "If he only knew what was ahead for him!" I wished I could somehow go back in time just so I could let the poor bastard—me—know it'd all work out better than he could ever imagine! That's when I had my first thoughts about trying to write again. I'd write a book to help others, just as I'd been helped. Initially I thought I'd use the journal entries, with a running commentary from my present perspective, but I junked that idea almost right away. Frankly, the idea of sharing some of that stuff was just too embarrassing for me—at least at that time. So I began to write about some of my experiences, describing the miracles and circumstances.

It was a struggle right from the start! My grammar and punctuation had suffered from years of inactivity—not that they'd ever been great to begin with. I seemed to have forgotten even the most basic rules. I made mistakes and errors that would have gotten me huge red circles on a composition if I'd still been in school. I misspelled, mistyped and generally fought with how to say what I wanted to say in that certain "right" way that would connect with someone. I was trying to find a way to get from my story to the lessons I'd learned, and then to the series of practices I'd used to help me get through that time. I wanted to return the favor and help some other poor schmuck know they weren't alone and that they could move on to a better life after all the pain and loss.

By the time I'd gotten to that hillside in 2001, I'd finished one book—the one I guess I had to write in order to be able to write the next one. I'd been sending that one to publishers and had already received my first half dozen rejections. I knew the book needed more work, and had begun to re-write the weak parts. By that day I suspected that *all* the parts were weak. Part of what led me to that hillside that day was my growing concern that I'd been deluding myself. After all, who was I kidding? I was no *real* writer. Maybe I'd just been taking advantage of the good fortune I'd been born into, and the fact my wife had a job with health benefits, thus allowing me to dabble at the variety of small jobs I did. On that day I was even questioning the motives behind the volunteer work I did. Maybe I'd been fooling myself about that as well. Maybe all this desire of mine to help was really a smoke screen to hide my deep seated guilt. And as you already know, I did guilt very well. Whenever I got started on that track I usually took it to the end of the line. So that's what was going on when I took my pad and pen to the hill overlooking the lake. Looking back, I believe what happened that day was due to the convergence of all this stuff—a "perfect storm" for me. After trying to solve my problem, after trying to think my way through things, after trying to come up with a clear answer and conclusion, I finally just put my pen down and sat there. I was depleted—empty, out of gas and ideas, and there, in that space, was the opportunity. Finally I had opened. And you know the rest.

My life has changed a good deal since that day. This writing thing has been a catalyst. As much as I've struggled with it, at times even walking away from it, I knew I had to finish what had been started, doubts and all. Although what happened on that hillside was extraordinary, I struggled with it and doubted its authenticity. I tried hard to find a logical explanation. You see, I love logic. I'm a "Trekkie" from way back., and the logical Mr. Spock was my favorite character. But logic failed me here. The truth was, I had no explanation. I had to accept that it was exactly what it appeared to be. That's what led to this book. So all that other writing had prepared me, as has everything else. While I was not instructed to write a book, it was made clear to me I had already been given what I needed to do what was asked of me.

Things continued to fall in place for me. Whenever I veered too far from the path, something always pulled me back to it. During those times when I felt doubtful about my own abilities to do this; when I'd believe I had nothing new to share, or that other smarter and more qualified people were already doing a better job at what I was trying to do; or when I'd ask myself yet one more time why you or anyone else would want to read a book written by some crackpot disguised as a regular guy, something *always* happened. A phone call came at exactly the right moment, with a question or an answer I needed to hear. I'd open a magazine or newspaper and there'd be something that would tie in with what I'd been trying to write about. I turned on the radio and heard someone speaking about the thing I was trying to say. I'd go out somewhere, and while I was driving words would come into my head—whole sentences and ideas, cohesive and complete! And I'd return to my computer, sit down, and have another go at it.

Just as I've changed and been changed by the writing I've done here, the world has also changed. When I'd first set out to write a book, terrorism was something that happened in far-away places, a Democrat was still in the White House, Gaza and Israel had not erupted into the center of violence it has become today. There were no 30 foot walls being built to keep Palestinians in, no U.S. troops in Afghanistan or Iraq. There's no denying this is a painful time. But let me remind you of what we've been told regarding pain. We know where pain can lead us if we face it. We humans are problem makers. But we are also problem solvers. And despite the seriousness of it all, I have great hope for our future. And remember, no matter how bleak things may appear, they will change. Everything is temporary. It really helps to know that!

It's an interesting thing to be able to have access to how one once thought and felt. Going back and reading my journal reminded me of how I once saw the world. It was a little like getting into a time machine for me. If anyone had ever told me that I'd see things as I do today I'd have told them they were crazy. As a matter of fact, the "me" of back then would think the "me" of today a bit of a wing-nut: a nice enough guy who has some crazy ideas about how life works and Who God is. What I do know is that I had believed certain things most of my life, they didn't change, and neither did I. They were absolutes to me. And those absolutes were often in conflict with what "was," keeping me constantly locked in the state of that which *should* be, at least according to me. This was a very hard way to live, and thank God things finally snapped.

Anyway, I know that I *have* changed, and my hope is that I will continue to do so; that I will continue to see and understand things in new ways, to remain open and willing to change.

Writing this book has been both a labor of love and a pain in the ass for me. As I told you right up front, I wanted to help others. That's been the love part of this thing. But doing this day in and day out, well, that's been the other part. Initially I thought this would be a big book—lots of pages, suggestions and maybe even a few exercises. I tend to be something of a wise guy, and even thought that I'd include some of that in the book to lighten things up a bit. But the more I wrote, the more I realized I needed less, not more. Fewer words. Fewer pages. The message was not a B-I-G and wordy message; it was brief and simple. Things do not need to be long and complicated in order to be profound. I have found the implications of this message to be just that. It is a message that has changed my life, and I know that change will continue as long as I stay connected to the message, reminding myself of its truth whenever I begin to forget. And sad to say, forgetting is part of being human, so I need to work at this.

But now, finally, the book is complete after all this time and all the typing, all the discarded chapters, all the rewrites and starting over, all the nonsense I've put myself through that I didn't have to put myself through—or maybe I did! Wherever the truth of that lies doesn't matter to me now. After all, I've made it! I've finally done it—the dance is over for me. No more avoidance, no more denial, no more trying to say things in a way that is understandable and won't peg me as some kind of nut. Writing this has relieved me of the worry of "what they might think," whoever the hell "they" might be. I've done what I was asked to do that day, I've delivered the message. It is now up to you. It's your turn to deliver the message.

So I'll leave you with this thought: when we're little kids we're really flexible, open to all kinds of adventure and experience. We can't wait to learn. Our minds take us to imaginary places, and we create all sorts of scenarios. We play all the time, and if it weren't for our moms or dads calling us in for supper or because it was getting dark out, we'd be outdoors caught up in our games until finally, spent and exhausted, we'd crawl inside to our beds, falling into that deep and delicious sleep that true play brings us. Our souls are satisfied and we sleep like the dead. I lost this sense as I grew. Most of us do. But this is what I've returned to.

I believe I am well on my way to my second childhood, and this time I know what to do with it! I will be more willing to take chances, more willing to appear foolish, more willing to admit I don't know, more willing to try new things. And much, much less willing to be anything other than who I really am. And this is my wish for you.

HEY! what are you doing inside on such a beautiful day? Close this book and get out there and have some fun!

And while you're at it, give someone a hand and a smile.

Recommended Reading

Russell, Peter. *From Science To God.* Sausalito, CA: Lightning Source, Inc.© 2000

Baumann, T. Lee, M.D. *God At The Speed Of Light.* Virginia Beach: A.R.E. Press © 2001

Wolf, Fred Alan, Ph.D. *The Dreaming Universe.* New York: Touchstone © 1994

978-0-595-34008-8
0-595-34008-3

Printed in the United States
48398LVS00008B/54

9 780595 340088